PROGRESSIVE THAI

Other Books by the Author:

Introduction to Thai Reading; Orchid Press, Bangkok 2007, 2018 (ISBN 978-974-524-211-1)

Co-authored with *Lucius Heijstee*:

Thai Signs and other Writings; Orchid Press, Bangkok 2008 (ISBN 978-974-524-104-6)

Uthai Thani: The Charm of a Hidden Gem; Thai Country Trails, Bangkok 2007 (ISBN 978-974-989-827-7)

PROGRESSIVE THAI

Rungrat Luanwarawat

Orchid Press

PROGRESSIVE THAI
Rungrat Luanwarawat

ORCHID PRESS
P.O. Box 19,
Yuttitham Post Office,
Bangkok 10907 Thailand
www.orchidbooks.com

Copyright © 2007, 2018 by Orchid Press. Protected by copyright under the terms of the International Copyright Union: all rights reserved. Except for fair use in book reviews, no part of this publication may be reproduced in any form or by any means, electronic or mechanical, including photocopying, recording, or by any information storage or retrieval system without prior permission in writing from the copyright holder.

ISBN: 978-974-524-213-5

CONTENTS

Topic	Page
About this book	vii
1. Phonetics	2
2. Grammar Introduction	11
3. Greetings and Useful Phrases	22
4. Nationality, Family and Career	28
5. Numbers	35
6. Eating Out	41
7. Shopping	56
8. Directions	70
9. Telling Time	81
10. Appointments	90
11. Invitation	100
12. Telephone Conversation	107
13. Housekeeping	115
14. Grooming	124
15. Medicine	133
16. Petty Crime	144
17. Key to Exercises	153

DOWNLOADING ACCOMPANYING AUDIO FILES

To download the MP-3 format audio files that are designed to accompany this text, please enter into your browser the following URL:

      http://www.orchidbooks.com/audio/index.html

You will be requested to enter your name, a valid Email address and a password.

      The password for this download is CJ?tv9p

The download will consist of a compressed folder. UnZIP the folder to locate the audio files within. These files may then be played on any current MP-3 compatible device or on your computer.

If there are any difficulties downloading or using the audio files, please contact Orchid Press for further assistance, at <downloadhelp@orchidbooks.com>

About This Book

Progressive Thai is designed for self study by students who have limited time but want to acquire a solid working knowledge of the Thai language. The course is also designed to be foundational—completion of the 16 progressive lessons will pave the way for higher-level learning. The book begins with an explanation of the Thai phonetic system, basic grammar rules, greetings, and useful phrases. These background sections are followed by situational topics. The vocabulary and grammar in each lesson builds on previous lessons, so students should read them in order.

Written in simple language, each lesson consists of interesting cultural tips, useful vocabulary, practical dialogue, concise grammar notes, usage tips, drills and exercises. The answer keys to the exercises are at the end of the book.

The cultural brief provides students with some relevant aspects of the Thai culture. Complicated words and phrases that appear in vocabulary lists and dialogues are marked with a superscript numeral; e.g. [1]. Their usage is explained in the Grammar Notes sections. A mini clock symbol represents a pause in the Dialogue section in the accompanying audio. The drills are meant for practicing in a limited context for fluency and pronunciation. The exercises are for testing the student's ability to deal with more realistic situations. To gain the most from this book, students should not proceed to the next lesson until they can do the exercises easily and correctly. Students are encouraged to practice what they learn from this book in real-life situations. The more practice they get applying the book's lessons in the real world, the quicker they will master basic vocabulary and pick up vital conversational skills. Such reinforcement is essential for language learning.

The Thai writing system is quite complex. Due to this complexity, I have excluded reading and writing from this beginning level self-learning book.

However, the book has included Thai script in every lesson. This will enable the students to gain some familiarity with the 'look' of Thai writing. Further, from the author's experience, it is common for some students to be able to read basic Thai without having basic conversational skills.

In the lessons, each sentence is both translated into English and transliterated into a modified form of the Roman alphabet. The author intends to have the English translation to be on a parallel with the Thai sayings. Thus, readers may find some of the English translations are more literal than normal spoken speech. The transliteration uses a few phonetic symbols where the Thai sound has no direct equivalent in the Roman alphabet. Because of such sounds, it is highly recommended that you rely on your ears by listening to the companion MP-3 audio track for the pronunciation.

Completion of this book will consume a few months of daily study and practice. Once you can practice all the exercises fluently, you are ready to assume the challenge of daily life in Thailand with the Thai language.

This book provides you with a solid working knowledge of the Thai spoken language. For those who would like to continue their studies, a higher-level book is now in preparation and should be available in the market soon.

I hope you enjoy this easy learning book and move up to a higher level.

Acknowledgement

I would like to thank my dearest editors, William Davis, Luciën Heijstee, David Schwartz and Tim Scherer, for their kind contributions. The book would not have been completed without their assistance. Thanks also to all of my students and friends at the US Embassy for their valuable comments and suggestions. They gave me inspiration and great support. I trust that this book will help them improve their Thai studies.

Keep learning....

Learning a tonal language can be painstaking but also fun. If you can hear the differences between the tones but can't say it, try this.

- *For a low tone, lower your face at the same time you lower your pitch.*
- *For a falling tone, move your face up and down according to the tone as you pronounce the word* or *pronounce the word as if there were an exclamation mark at the end – e.g.: "No!",*
- *For a high tone, move your face up while raising your pitch.*
- *For a rising tone, face down and quickly up while pronouncing the word. Or pronounce the word as if there were a question mark at the end – e.g.: "No?"*

Some may find this method of practicing tonal pronunciation rather unusual. However, it has proven beneficial to many students.

Practice this at home or with native speakers until you can pronounce the 5 tones correctly. Once you master the 5-tone pronunciation, you need not move your face around any longer.

1. Phonetics

CONSONANTS

The Thai Language contains 44 consonants, two of which are obsolete. Some of the consonants represent the same sound and some are more widely used than others. Of the 44 consonants, there are only 21 initial sounds and 8 final sounds.

Note that many Thais tend to substitute the 'l' for the 'r' sound. In the case where the 'r' is a part of an initial consonant cluster, some people may leave out the 'r' sound completely.

The table below shows a list of phonetic symbols representing consonant sounds that will be used in this book. For example, when 'g' is spelt as an initial consonant, it always represents the sound 'g' as in 'go', not in 'gin'.

21 Initial Sounds	Phonetic Symbols		44 Thai Initial Consonants
1	g	(as in 'go')	ก
2	k	(as in 'king')	ข ค ฆ ฃ ฅ (ฃ ฅ are obsolete)
3	ng	(as in 'singing')	ง
4	j	(as in 'joy')	จ
5	ch	(as in 'chin')	ช ฉ ฌ
6	s	(as in 'say')	ซ ส ษ ศ
7	y	(as in 'year')	ย ญ
8	d	(as in 'day')	ด ฎ
9	dt	(pronounced together similar to 'stand')	ต ฏ
10	t	(as in 'tap')	ท ฒ ฑ ธ ถ ฐ
11	n	(as in 'none')	น ณ

12	b	(as in 'bay')	บ
13	bp	(pronounced together, similar to 'spy')	ป
14	p	(as in 'pie')	พ ภ ผ
15	f	(as in 'fan')	ฟ ฝ
16	m	(as in 'may')	ม
17	r	(as in 'ray')	ร
18	l	(as in 'lay')	ล ฬ
19	w	(as in 'way')	ว
20	h	(as in 'hen')	ห ฮ
21	(none)	When the nitial consonant's sound is silent.	อ

The Thai final sounds are quite limited and only some consonants are used. The final 'p', 't', 'k' sounds are not released as in English but are 'swallowed' at the end.

8 Final Sounds	Phonetic Symbols		Thai Final Consonants
1	k	(as in 'back')	ก ข ค ฆ
2	ng	(as in 'sing')	ง
3	m	(as in 'ham')	ม
4	t	(as in 'bat')	ท ฑ ฒ ธ ถ ฐ จ ช ษ ศ ส ด ฏ ซ ด ต ฎ ฏ
5	n	(as in 'man')	น ณ ญ ร ล ฬ
6	p	(as in 'cap')	พ ภ ฟ บ ป
7	w	(or short 'oo', similar to cow)	ว
8	y	(or short 'ii', similar to 'boy')	ย

VOWELS

There are 32 vowels in the Thai language. The vowels can be divided into 3 groups; monophthong (short & long vowels), diphthong (short & long vowels) and extra vowels. Some of the vowels are obsolete or rarely used. Special attention must be given to the phonetic symbols in comparison with their English equivalent sounds as shown below. For example, when 'ii' is spelt as a vowel, it always represents the sound 'ii' as in 't<u>ea</u>', not as in 'p<u>ie</u>'.

The underlined phonetics symbols represent short vowels. The short and long vowels basically represent the same sound, only one is shorter than the other.

Monophthong				
Short Vowels		Long Vowels		
Phonetics Symbols	Thai Vowels	Phonetics Symbols	Thai Vowels	Equivalent Sounds
<u>ah</u>	_ ะ	ah	_า	'baht'
<u>i</u>	◌ิ	ii	◌ี	'tea'
<u>eu</u>	◌ึ	eu	◌ื	sounds as you have a hiccup
<u>oo</u>	◌ุ	oo	◌ู	'do'
<u>eh</u>	เ_ะ	eh	เ_	'ray'
<u>ae</u>	แ_ะ	ae	แ_	'fair'
<u>oh</u>	โ_ะ	oh	โ_	'so'
<u>aw</u>	เ_าะ	aw	_อ	'saw'
<u>e(r)</u>	เ_อะ	e(r)	เ_อ	'her' but without 'r' rolling sound

Diphthong				
Short Vowels		Long Vowels		
Phonetics Symbols	Thai Vowels	Phonetics Symbols	Thai Vowels	Equivalent Sounds
ia	เ◌ียะ	ia	เ◌ีย	'dear' but without the 'r' rolling sound. The short vowel is a combination of 'i' and '<u>ah</u>'. The long vowel is from 'ii' and 'ah'
ua	◌ัวะ	ua	◌ัว	'poor' but without the 'r' rolling sound. The short vowel is a combination of '<u>oo</u>' and '<u>ah</u>'. The long vowel is from 'oo' and 'ah'.
eua	เ◌ือะ	eua	เ◌ือ	The short vowel is a combination of '<u>eu</u>' and '<u>ah</u>'. The long vowel is from 'eu' and 'ah'.

Extra Vowels		
Phonetics Symbols	Thai Vowels	Equivalent Sounds
am	◌ำ	'pump'
ai	ไ◌, ใ◌	'tight'
ao	เ◌า	'out' without 't' at the end
r<u>eu</u>	ฤ	The combination of 'r' and '<u>eu</u>'
reu	ฤๅ	This is obsolete.
l<u>eu</u>	ฦ	This is obsolete.
leu	ฦๅ	This is obsolete.

Note: Additionally, there are a few combinations of some vowels with consonants 'ว' or 'ย' that are widely used and worth noting. When these two consonants appear as final consonants, they sound like vowel endings. Observe the phonetic symbols and the explanations below. Pronounce the combination of these two sounds separately but with no pause between them. Later in this book, you will come across the same phonetic symbols but with an underline, they represent shorter sound than the ones below.

Phonetics Symbols	Thai Vowels	Explanation
ah-ii	_ าย	The combination of 'ah' and 'ii'.
ah-oo	_ าว	The combination of 'ah' and 'oo'.
aew	แ _ ว	The combination of 'ae' and 'oo'.
aw-ii	_ อย	The combination of 'aw' and 'ii'.
oh-ii	โ _ ย	The combination of 'oh' and 'ii'.
eua-ii	เ _ ือย	The combination of 'eua' and 'ii'.
e(r)-ii	เ _ ย	The combination of 'e(r)' and 'ii'.
eh-oo	เ _ ว	The combination of 'eh' and 'oo'.
iaw	เ _ ียว	The combination of 'ia' and 'oo'.

The Thai language is a tonal language. There are 5 tones including mid, low, falling, high and rising. No single word is pronounced in all five. Most of the words are pronounced in two or three tones. Different tones carry different meanings. In some cases, even though your tone is incorrect, the context helps overcoming the tone barrier.

The mid tone is the normal pitch of voice. The low tone is lower than normal pitch. The falling tone begins at a high pitch, then drops lower. The high tone is higher than normal pitch. The rising begins at a low pitch, and then rises sharply.

Tones	Mid	Low	Falling	High	Rising
Phonetic Symbols		`	^	´	ˇ
Examples	gah	gàh	gâh	gáh	gǎh

DRILLS

1. Practice consonants & vowels pronunciation by repeating after the audio.

   A. ah gahn อาการ (*symptom*)　　B. ah kahn อาคาร (*building*)
   C. gài ไก่ (*chicken*)　　D. kài ไข่ (*egg*)
   E. pah พา (*to bring*)　　F. bpah ปา (*to throw*)
   G. john จน (*poor*)　　H. chohn ชน (*to bump*)
   I. bâh บ้า (*crazy*)　　J. bpâh ป้า (*aunt*)
   K. bpêuan เปื้อน (*stain*)　　L. pêuan เพื่อน (*friend*)
   M. dii ดี (*good*)　　N. dtii ตี (*to hit*)
   O. bìt บิด (*to twist*)　　P. bpìt ปิด (*to close*)
   Q. pèht เผ็ด (*spicy*)　　R. bpèht เป็ด (*duck*)
   S. tah ทา (*to smear*)　　T. dtah ตา (*eye*)
   U. tah-ii ทาย (*to guess*)　　V. dtah-ii ตาย (*to die*)
   W. kahng คาง (*chin*)　　X. gahng กาง (*to open up*)
   Y. ngahn งาน (*work*)　　Z. nahn นาน (*long time*)

2. Practice tones pronunciation by repeating after the audio.

   A. mah มา (*to come*)　　B. máh ม้า (*horse*)
   C. máh ม้า (*horse*)　　D. mǎh หมา (*dog*)

E. mǎw หมอ (*doctor*)
F. mâw หม้อ (*pot*)
G. glai ไกล (*far*)
H. glâi ใกล้ (*near*)
I. paw พอ (*enough*)
J. pâw พ่อ (*father*)
K. nîi นี่ (*this*)
L. nǐi หนี (*to flee*)
M. nah นา (*farm*)
N. nâh หน้า (*face*)
O. tahm ทำ (*to do*)
P. tâhm ถ้ำ (*cave*)
Q. yah ยา (*medicine*)
R. yàh อย่า (*Don't!*)
S. róo รู้ (*to know*)
T. roo รู (*hole*)
U. hâh ห้า (*five*)
V. hǎh หา (*to look for*)
W. b<u>oh</u>n บน (*on*)
X. bòhn บ่น (*to complain*)
Y. kòo ขู่ (*to threaten*)
Z. kôo คู่ (*pair*)

EXERCISES

1. Listen to the audio and choose the right answer.

   A1. máe แม้ (*though*)
   A2. mâe แม่ (*mother*)
   B1. dtah ตา (*eye*)
   B2. dtàe แต่ (*but*)
   C1. pìt ผิด (*wrong*)
   C2. bpìt ปิด (*close*)
   D1. sêua เสื้อ (*shirt*)
   D2. sěua เสือ (*tiger*)
   E1. máh ม้า (*horse*)
   E2. mǎh หมา (*dog*)
   F1. ch<u>âh</u>ng ช่าง (*handy-man*)
   F2. cháhng ช้าง (*elephant*)
   G1. l<u>oh</u>ng ลง (*down*)
   G2. lǒhng หลง (*lost the way*)
   H1. fáh ฟ้า (*sky*)
   H2. fǎh ฝา (*lid*)
   I1. mii มี (*to have*)
   I2. mǐi หมี (*bear*)
   J1. bpii ปี (*year*)
   J2. pǐi ผี (*ghost*)
   K1. kâh-oo ข้าว (*rice*)
   K2. kǎh-oo ขาว (*white*)
   L1. kâi ไข้ (*fever*)
   L2. kài ไข่ (*egg*)
   M1. wǎen แหวน (*ring*)
   M2. w<u>ae</u>n แว่น (*glasses*)

2. Listen to the audio and add the correct tone mark.

A. law	B. nah
C. glai	D. glai
E. glua	F. hiw
G. dah	H. gaew
I. j<u>ah</u>m	J. jai
K. bahn	L. rian
M. neua-ii	N. n<u>ah</u>t
O. meut	P. nahm
Q. h<u>aw</u>ng	R. kit
S. leum	T. k<u>ah</u>p
U. n<u>ah</u>ng	V. nawn
W. l<u>eh</u>n	X. rah-ii
Y. sii	Z. hah

Thai people are well-known for their tolerance and understanding. When a foreigner attempts to overcome the Thai language barrier, the Thai may smile or laugh. However, this is not a sign of offence. Rather, it is a gesture of appreciation. Thai people in general are pleased to hear foreigners speak, or attempting to speak their language. They always compliment foreigners' language skills no matter how limited they may be. In fact, you know you have arrived at a very competent speaking level when Thai people stop complimenting your language skills!

2. Grammar Introduction

Thai grammar is much less complicated compared to English. There are not many rules and inflections. The principal rules of communicative grammar are as follows:

1. The pronoun is a complicated subject in the Thai language. Pronouns and their object forms are the same word. Thais use pronouns differently and variably according to their status, age, gender, position, profession and so forth.

Apart from using different pronouns, Thai women and Thai men use different polite particles to end a sentence. The word 'kàh' (low tone) ค่ะ in a statement and 'káh' (high tone) คะ in a question are used by women. Men only have one word of this kind, 'kráhp' ครับ. When Thais address each other, they will use the person's first name preceded by the word 'khun' คุณ (similar to 'Mr', 'Ms') or the position of a person, or another status like brother, sister, etc. It is also a polite form of the pronoun 'you'.

In informal circumstances, Thais often address each other by using a family status pronoun even though they are not related. You may hear a Thai address his senior co-worker as 'pîi' พี่ meaning 'older sibling'. In colloquial Thai, it is customary to leave out the pronouns 'you' and 'I', prepositions and some other words; provided that the intended meaning of the sentence is expressed adequately.

koon	คุณ	You
pŏhm	ผม	I (male), me
(dì) cháhn	ดิฉัน	I, me (female adult)

11

nŏo	หนู	I, me (junior, usually girls) You (used to call a child)
káo	เค้า	he, she, him, her
pûak káo	พวกเค้า	they, them
rao เรา, pûak rao	พวกเรา	we, us

Ex. A: Sàh wàht dii kàh, koon măw.
   สวัสดีค่ะ คุณหมอ Hello, doctor.
   B: Sàh wàht dii kráhp koon dtóok.
   สวัสดีครับ คุณตุ๊ก Hello, khun Took.

2. Possession is indicated by adding the word 'kăwng' ของ (*of*) after a noun and in front of a pronoun, but this is often omitted.

| róht | รถ | car |
| bâhn | บ้าน | house, home |

Ex. Róht (kăwng) pŏhm.
   รถ(ของ)ผม My car.
Ex. Bâhn (kăwng) rao.
   บ้าน(ของ)เรา Our house.

3. There are no articles in front of nouns and no distinction in form between the singular and plural. Plurality is indicated by the context or additional words.

mii	มี	to have
lôok	ลูก	one's child/children
kohn	คน	person, classifier for person

Ex. Káo mii lôok.
   เค้ามีลูก He/she has kid/kids.

Ex. Káo mii lôok sìi kohn.
เค้ามีลูกสี่คน He/she has 4 kids.

4. Verbs in Thai do not change form in correlatoin with changes in nouns, pronouns, or time. However, the context usually makes it clear which interpretation is intended, sometimes by the use of extra words. The time or state of an action is indicated by the use of time words and/or particles. The future tense is indicated by putting the word 'jàh' จะ (*will*) in front of the verb.

châwp	ชอบ	to like
tîi nîi	ที่นี่	here
tîi	ที่	at (or 'in', a preposition to indicate location)
tahm ngahn	ทำงาน	to work
groong têhp	กรุงเทพ	Bangkok
dtawn níi	ตอนนี้	presently
mêua gàwn níi	เมื่อก่อนนี้	previously

Ex. Káo châwp tîi nîi.
เค้าชอบที่นี่ He/she likes it here.

Ex. Pûak káo châwp tîi nîi.
พวกเค้าชอบที่นี่ They like it here.

Ex. Dtawn níi pŏhm tahm ngahn tîi groong têhp.
ตอนนี้ผมทำงานที่กรุงเทพ Presently, I work in Bangkok.

Ex. Mêua gàwn níi pŏhm tahm ngahn tîi groong têhp.
เมื่อก่อนนี้ผมทำงานที่กรุงเทพ Previously I worked in Bangkok.

Ex. Pŏhm jàh tahm ngahn tîi groong têhp.
ผมจะทำงานที่กรุงเทพ I will work in Bangkok.

5. Adjectives, modifiers and specific names come after the nouns they modify, not before as in English.

níi	นี้	this
n<u>á</u>hn	นั้น	that
sŭay	สวย	beautiful
bpr<u>à</u>h têht	ประเทศ	country
pah săh	ภาษา	language
rohng raem	โรงแรม	hotel
l<u>é</u>hk	เล็ก	small

Ex. Bpr<u>à</u>h têht níi.
   ประเทศนี้ This country
Ex. K<u>oh</u>n sŭay.
   คนสวย A beautiful person
Ex. Pah săh tai
   ภาษาไทย Thai language
Ex. Rohng raem l<u>é</u>hk.
   โรงแรมเล็ก A small hotel

6. The basic English structure: Subject + 'to be' + adjective, when converted into Thai, 'to be' is always omitted.

s<u>à</u>h àht	สะอาด	clean
ah gàht	อากาศ	weather
y<u>eh</u>n	เย็น	cool
ah hăhn	อาหาร	food
pèht	เผ็ด	spicy

Ex. Bâhn s<u>à</u>h àht.
   บ้านสะอาด The house is clean.

Ex. Ah gàht y<u>e</u>hn.
อากาศเย็น The weather is cool.

Ex. Ah hăhn pèht.
อาหารเผ็ด The food is spicy.

7. The basic structure of a Thai sentence is Subject + Verb + Object.

yòo	อยู่	to live, to stay
bp<u>e</u>hn	เป็น	to be + noun
l<u>ê</u>hn	เล่น	to play

Ex. Káo yòo chiang mài.
เค้าอยู่เชียงใหม่ He/she lives in Chiang Mai.

Ex. K<u>oo</u>n bp<u>e</u>hn k<u>o</u>hn tai.
คุณเป็นคนไทย You are Thai.

Ex. Káo l<u>ê</u>hn bpian noh.
เค้าเล่นเปียโน He/she plays piano.

8. Statements and questions are of the same pattern. A question can be formed by adding a question word, usually at the end of the sentence.

arai? อะไร?	What?
tîi năi? ที่ไหน?	Where?
mêua rai? เมื่อไร?	When?
krai? ใคร?	Who?
y<u>a</u>hng ngai? ยังไง?	How?
tâo rai? เท่าไร?	How much?
t<u>a</u>hm mai? ทำไม?	Why?
mái? มั้ย?	Do?, Does?, Is?, Am?, Are?
r<u>é</u>u bplàh-oo? รึเปล่า?	Do?, Does?, Is?, Am?, Are?

dâi mái? ได้มั้ย?		Can?
lĕ(r) เหรอ?		Right?
châi mái? ใช่มั้ย?		Right?

The interrogative sentences below are transformed from the statements shown in No.7. Observe the word order of the following questions and you will see that every sentence follows the basic structure: Subject + Verb + Object.

Ex. Káo yòo tîi năi?
     เค้าอยู่ที่ไหน? Where is he/she?

Ex. K<u>oo</u>n bp<u>eh</u>n k<u>oh</u>n arai?
     คุณเป็นคนอะไร? What nationality are you?

Ex. Káo l<u>êh</u>n arai?
     เค้าเล่นอะไร? What does he/she play?

Ex. Krai l<u>êh</u>n bpian noh?
     ใครเล่นเปียนโน? Who plays piano?

Ex. Káo l<u>êh</u>n bpian noh r<u>éu</u> bplàh-oo?
     เค้าเล่นเปียนโนรึเปล่า? Does he/she play piano?

Ex. Káo l<u>êh</u>n bpian noh dâi mái?
     เค้าเล่นเปียนโนได้มั้ย? Can he/she play piano?

9. A negative sentence is formed by putting a negative word in front of the verb; 'mâi' ไม่ (*not*), or 'mâi dâi' ไม่ได้ (*did not, not being*).

dèum	ดื่ม	to drink
gah fae	กาแฟ	coffee
<u>ah</u>ng grìt	อังกฤษ	English
àhn	อ่าน	to read
rian	เรียน	to study

Ex. Rao mâi dèum gah fae.
เราไม่ดื่มกาแฟ We don't drink coffee.

Ex. Káo mâi dâi rian.
เค้าไม่ได้เรียน He/She didn't study.

Ex. Pŏhm mâi dâi bpehn kohn ahng grìt.
ผมไม่ได้เป็นคนอังกฤษ I am not British.

If 'mâi dâi' ไม่ได้ appears after the verb or at the end of the sentence, it means 'can't'.

Ex. Pŏhm pôot pah săh tai mâi dâi.
ผมพูดภาษาไทยไม่ได้ I can't speak Thai.

Ex. Pŏhm àhn pah săh ahng grìt mâi dâi.
ผมอ่านภาษาอังกฤษไม่ได้ I can't read English

10. Unlike English, when a negative word qualifies an adjective or an adverb, it is usually placed between the noun and the adjective or between the verb and the adverb.

yài	ใหญ่	big
ráwn	ร้อน	hot
wahn níi	วันนี้	today
kàhp róht	ขับรถ	to drive
reh-oo	เร็ว	fast
pôot	พูด	to speak
cháht	ชัด	clear, clearly

Ex. Bpràh têht mâi yài.
ประเทศไม่ใหญ่ Not a big country.

Ex. Wahn níi mâi ráwn.
วันนี้ไม่ร้อน Today is not hot.

Ex. Di cháhn kàhp róht mâi reh-oo.
ดิฉันขับรถไม่เร็ว I don't drive fast.

Ex. Káo pôot mâi ch<u>á</u>ht.
เค้าพูดไม่ชัด He/She doesn't speak clearly.

ADDITIONAL BASIC VOCABULARY

róht	รถ	car
mâhk	มาก	very, much
dii	ดี	good
dii mâhk	ดีมาก	very good
làw	หล่อ	handsome
năh-oo	หนาว	cold
gèhng	เก่ง	skillful, capable
cháh	ช้า	slow
t<u>a</u>hm	ทำ	to do
t<u>a</u>hm ah hăhn	ทำอาหาร	to cook
tahn / gin	ทาน / กิน	to eat
t<u>a</u>hm kwahm s<u>à</u>h àht	ทำความสะอาด	to clean
chûay	ช่วย	to help
bpai	ไป	to go
mah	มา	to come
de(r)n	เดิน	to walk
doo	ดู	to look
h<u>ĕ</u>hn	เห็น	to see
f<u>a</u>hng	ฟัง	to listen
tîi n<u>â</u>hn	ที่นั่น	there
nge(r)n	เงิน	money

DRILLS

1. Practice rule No.3 by replacing the pronoun in each sentence with the bracketed word.

    A. Káo mii bâhn เค้ามีบ้าน He/She has a house/houses. (pûak káo พวกเค้า)

    B. Pŏhm mii róht ผมมีรถ I have a car/cars. (rao เรา)

    C. Di cháhn mii lôok ดิฉันมีลูก I have a child/childern. (koon คุณ)

    D. Rao mii nge(r)n เรามีเงิน We have money. (cháhn ฉัน)

2. Practice rule No. 4 by adding 'jàh' จะ (will) in front of the verb.

    A. Pŏhm bpai tahm ngahn ผมไปทำงาน I go to work.

    B. Krai mah tîi nîi? ใครมาที่นี่? Who comes here?

    C. Koon tahm arai? คุณทำอะไร? What do you do?

    D. Káo doo tii wii เค้าดูทีวี He/She watches TV.

3. Practice rule No. 8 by changing the sentence: 'Káo rian pah săh tai tîi Chiang Mai' เค้าเรียนภาษาไทยที่เชียงใหม่ *She/He studies Thai in Chiang Mai.*, into questions using the given question words as follows.

    A. krai? ใคร? Who?

    B. arai? อะไร? What?

    C. tîi năi? ที่ไหน? Where?

    D. réu bplàh-oo? รึเปล่า? or not?

EXERCISES

1. How do you say the following phrases/sentences in Thai?

    A. His home.

    B. His home is big.

C. Is his home big?
D. I saw you.
E. What did you see?
F. Thailand is hot.
G. Thailand is not cold.
H. Small country.
I. He goes to work.
J. How does he go to work?
K. They are cold.
L. They are not hot.
M. Are you cold?

2. Translate the following sentences into English.
    A. Rao j<u>àh</u> yòo tîi nîi. เราจะอยู่ที่นี่
    B. K<u>oo</u>n j<u>àh</u> yòo tîi năi? คุณจะอยู่ที่ไหน?
    C. Ah gàht ráwn. อากาศร้อน
    D. Ah gàht tîi nîi ráwn. อากาศที่นี่ร้อน
    E. T<u>ah</u>m ngahn g<u>èh</u>ng. ทำงานเก่ง
    F. Káo t<u>ah</u>m ngahn g<u>èh</u>ng. เค้าทำงานเก่ง
    G. Káo t<u>ah</u>m ngahn mâi g<u>èh</u>ng. เค้าทำงานไม่เก่ง
    H. Bpai tîi n<u>âh</u>n. ไปที่นั่น
    I. K<u>oo</u>n j<u>àh</u> bpai tîi n<u>âh</u>n châi mái? คุณจะไปที่นั่นใช่มั้ย?
    J. K<u>oo</u>n j<u>àh</u> bpai tîi-n<u>âh</u>n r<u>éu</u>-bplàh-oo? คุณจะไปที่นั่นรึเปล่า?
    K. T<u>ah</u>m-mai k<u>oo</u>n j<u>àh</u> bpai tîi-n<u>âh</u>n? ทำไมคุณจะไปที่นั่น?
    L. Krai j<u>àh</u> bpai tîi-n<u>âh</u>n? ใครจะไปที่นั่น?
    M. Káo yòo tîi-n<u>âh</u>n. เค้าอยู่ที่นั่น

'Sawaddii' is used for both greeting and taking leave at any time of day or night. Once you know a person, the greeting form may be a phrase such as:'Where are you going?'; 'What are you doing?'; 'What are you eating?' Sometimes such questions are more an informal greeting than an attempt to find out about a friend's immediate destination or action. Small talk is mostly about one's background. This type of information inquiry is not considered intrusive.

The 'wai' is used for several reasons. It is a sign of greeting, made by raising both hands, palms joined, to a position lightly touching the body somewhere between the chest and the forehead. The higher the hands are raised, the greater the respect and courtesy conveyed. The person who is junior in age or social rank is the first one who gives the 'wai'. The senior returns the greeting by 'waiing' back with the hands raised no higher than the chest. This form of greeting is almost always accompanied by a smile and by saying 'sawaddii'.

3. Greetings and Useful Phrases

VOCABULARY

Sàh wàht dii	สวัสดี	Hello, bye
Kàwp koon	ขอบคุณ	Thank you[1]
Kăw tôht	ขอโทษ	excuse me, sorry (apologize)[2]
Mâi bpehn rai	ไม่เป็นไร	It's OK. Never mind.[3]
Yin dii	ยินดี	My pleasure; You are welcome.[4]
Bpai gàwn náh	ไปก่อนนะ	I've got to go now.
Láew je(r) gahn	แล้วเจอกัน	See you.
Póhp gahn mài	พบกันใหม่	See you (more formal)
Arai náh?	อะไรนะ?	What did you say?
Bpehn yahng ngai (bâhng)?	เป็นยังไง(บ้าง)?	How are you?[5]
Sáh bah-ii dii mái?	สบายดีมั้ย?	How are you? (more formal)
Sáh bah-ii dii.	สบายดี	(I am) fine.
Rêua-ii rêua-ii	เรื่อยๆ	So so.[6]
Láew koon làh?	แล้วคุณล่ะ?	And you?[7]
Bpai năi?	ไปไหน?	Where are (you) going?
Pôot pah săh tai mâi dâi	พูดภาษาไทยไม่ได้	(I) can't speak Thai.
Pôot pah săh tai dâi nít nàw-ii	พูดภาษาไทยได้นิดหน่อย	(I) can speak Thai a little bit.

Chûay pôot cháh cháh nàw-ii   ช่วยพูดช้าๆหน่อย   Please speak slowly.

Pôot pah săh ahng grìt dâi mái?   พูดภาษาอังกฤษได้มั้ย?   Can (you) speak English?

Mâi kâo jai   ไม่เข้าใจ   (I) don't understand.

Mâi ao   ไม่เอา   (I) don't want (it).

DIALOGUE 1

A: Sàh wàht dii kráhp koon daeng.
สวัสดีครับคุณแดง Hello khun Daeng.

B: Sàh wàht dii kàh koon jim. Bpehn yahng ngai bâhng káh?
สวัสดีค่ะคุณจิม เป็นยังไงบ้างคะ? Hello khun Jim. How are you?

A: Pŏhm sàh bah-ii dii, láew koon làh kráhp?
ผมสบายดี แล้วคุณล่ะครับ? I am fine, and you?

B: Rêua-ii rêua-ii kàh.
เรื่อยๆค่ะ So-so.

A: Arai náh kráhp?
อะไรนะครับ? What did you say?

B: Rêua-ii rêua-ii kàh.
เรื่อยๆค่ะ So-so.

A: Kăw tôht, pŏhm mâi kâo jai kráhp.
ขอโทษ ผมไม่เข้าใจครับ Sorry, I don't understand.

B: Mâi bpehn rai kàh. Bpai gàwn náh káh.
ไม่เป็นไรค่ะ ไปก่อนนะคะ Never mind. I've got to go now.

A: Láew je(r) gahn kráhp.
แล้วเจอกันครับ See you.

DIALOGUE 2

A: Koon jim, bpai năi káh?
คุณจิม ไปไหนคะ? Khun Jim, where are you going?

B: Pŏhm mâi châi koon jim kráhp.
ผมไม่ใช่คุณจิมครับ I am not khun Jim.

A: Kăw tôht kàh.
ขอโทษค่ะ I am sorry.

B: Mâi bpehn rai kráhp.
ไม่เป็นไรครับ It's OK.

GRAMMAR NOTES

1. When thanking someone younger or lower in rank or status, Thais sometimes use 'kàwp jai' ขอบใจ instead of 'kàwp koon' ขอบคุณ.

2. Use 'kăw tôht' ขอโทษ when you want to interrupt someone or when you want to apologize.

3. 'Mâi bpehn rai' ไม่เป็นไร conveys several meanings. It is equivalent to 'It's OK'; 'Never mind'; 'It doesn't matter'; 'Not at all'. Use this phrase in respond to 'kăw tôht' ขอโทษ or 'kàwp koon' ขอบคุณ.

4. 'Yin dii' ยินดี is similar to 'my pleasure'. It is a polite way of responding to 'kàwp koon' ขอบคุณ.

5. 'Bpehn yahng ngai?' เป็นยังไง? is used to ask someone's well-being. You can also use the same pattern to ask about other things.

   Ex. Ah meh ri gah bpehn yahng ngai?
   อเมริกาเป็นยังไง? How is America? (Big, small, hot, cold, etc.)

6. 'Rêua-ii rêua-ii' เรื่อยๆ is equivalent to 'so so'. It is used to express the well-being in the areas of health, business, and

relationships. To express the 'so-so' quality of something, say 't<u>ah</u>m m<u>ah</u> dah' ธรรมดา or 'y<u>ah</u>ng ngáhn, y<u>ah</u>ng ngáhn' ยังงั้น ยังงั้น.

⁷ When you want to respond with the same question, say 'láew k<u>oo</u>n l<u>à</u>h?' แล้วคุณล่ะ?

DRILLS

1. Practice greeting by asking ' ___ s<u>à</u>h bah-ii dii mái?' ___สบายดีมั้ย? *How are/is___?* by completing the sentence using the followings words.

A. <u>Koon</u>	คุณ	you
B. P<u>ah</u>n r<u>ah</u> yah k<u>oo</u>n	ภรรยาคุณ	your wife
C. S<u>ă</u>h mii k<u>oo</u>n	สามีคุณ	your husband
D. Lôok k<u>oo</u>n	ลูกคุณ	your child
E. K<u>oo</u>n pâw	คุณพ่อ	your father
F. K<u>oo</u>n mâe	คุณแม่	your mother
G. Faen k<u>oo</u>n	แฟนคุณ	your girl-friend
		your boy-friend

2. Practice '___bp<u>eh</u>n y<u>ah</u>ng ngai?' ___เป็นยังไง? *How are/is___?* by completing the phrase using the followings words.

A. J<u>à</u>h dt<u>òo</u> j<u>à</u>hk	จตุจักร	Jatujak
B. P<u>á</u>ht t<u>ah</u> yah	พัทยา	Pattaya
C. Ngahn	งาน	work
D. Ngahn líang	งานเลี้ยง	party
E. Mêua wahn-níi	เมื่อวานนี้	yesterday
F. N<u>ă</u>hng	หนัง	movie
G. Ah h<u>ă</u>hn	อาหาร	food

EXERCISES

1. How do you respond to the following phrases.

    A. Kàwp koon kàh.   ขอบคุณค่ะ
    B. Kăw tôht kàh.   ขอโทษค่ะ
    C. Sàh wàht dii kàh   สวัสดีค่ะ
    D. Bpai gàwn náh kráhp   ไปก่อนนะครับ
    E. Láew je(r) gahn kàh   แล้วเจอกันค่ะ

2. Match the left column to the right column.

    A. Sàh bah-ii dii mái káh?   1. Mâi bpehn rai kráhp.
       สบายดีมั้ยค่ะ?   ไม่เป็นไรครับ

    B. Kàwp koon kàh.   2. Yin dii kráhp.
       ขอบคุณค่ะ   ยินดีครับ

    C. Kăw tôht kàh.   3. Rêua-ii rêua-ii kráhp.
       ขอโทษค่ะ   เรื่อยๆ ครับ

    D. Bpai năi káh?   4. Láew je(r) gahn kráhp.
       ไปไหนคะ?   แล้วเจอกันครับ

    E. Bpai gàwn náh káh.   5. Bpai tahm ngaan kráhp.
       ไปก่อนนะคะ   ไปทำงานครับ

When Thai people are introduced to one another, last names are usually not included. Thai surnames are never used on their own, in the way Westerners are accustomed to doing. Sometimes Thai people who have known each other for years don't know each other's surnames.

Thai names are given by monks, fortune tellers or parents of a new-born baby. Parents choose auspicious names, often suggested by a monk or a fortune-teller for luck. Every Thai name carries a positive meaning, such as 'good', 'holy', 'auspicious', 'famous', 'victory'. Nearly every Thai has a nickname by which they are always known among their family and friends. Sometimes the nickname is a shortened form of the real name. People occasionally identify one another based on appearance, such as 'tall', 'fat', 'thin' and often these words become one's nickname, without being considered offensive (usually).

4. Nationality, Family and Career

VOCABULARY

chêu	ชื่อ	name
chêu lêhn	ชื่อเล่น	nickname
nahm sah goon	นามสกุล	last name
bpehn	เป็น	to be[1]
pôo yĭng	ผู้หญิง	female (human)
pôo chah-ii	ผู้ชาย	male (human)
krâwp krua	ครอบครัว	family
pâw	พ่อ	father
mâe	แม่	mother
bpòo	ปู่	father's father
yâh	ย่า	father's mother
dtah	ตา	mother's father
yah-ii	ยาย	mother's mother
lôok	ลูก	one's child, children
lôok chah-ii	ลูกชาย	son
lôok săh-oo	ลูกสาว	daughter
pîi chah-ii	พี่ชาย	older brother
pîi săh-oo	พี่สาว	older sister
náwng chah-ii	น้องชาย	younger brother
náwng săh-oo	น้องสาว	younger sister
dèhk	เด็ก	child, children (in general)[2]

loong	ลุง	uncle
bpâh	ป้า	aunt
lăhn	หลาน	grandchild, niece, nephew
săh mii	สามี	husband
pahn rah yah	ภรรยา	wife
pêuan	เพื่อน	friend
pôo yài	ผู้ใหญ่	adult
ah yóo	อายุ	age
bpii	ปี	year
kùap	ขวบ	year (classifier)[3]
săhn châht	สัญชาติ	nationality
ah chîip	อาชีพ	profession, career
ngahn	งาน	work, job
tahm ngahn	ทำงาน	to work
rohng pah yah bahn	โรงพยาบาล	hospital
rohng rian	โรงเรียน	school
baw ri sàht	บริษัท	company
jàhk	จาก	from

DIALOGUE

A: Kăw tôht kàh, koon chêu arai káh?[4]
   ขอโทษค่ะ คุณชื่ออะไรคะ? Excuse me, what is your name?

B: Pŏhm chêu jim kráhp.
   ผมชื่อจิมครับ My name is Jim.

A: Nahm sah goon arai káh?
   นามสกุลอะไรคะ? What is your last name?

B: Hae rîi kráhp.
แฮรี่ครับ Harry.

A: Koon bpehn kohn arai káh?
คุณเป็นคนอะไรคะ?

Or: Koon săhn châht arai káh?
คุณสัญชาติอะไรคะ? What nationality are you?

B: Bpehn kohn ah meh ri gahn kráhp. Pŏhm mah jàhk niw yàwk เป็นคนอเมริกันครับ ผมมาจากนิวยอร์ค I am American. I come from New York.

A: Koon tahm ngahn tîi năi káh?
คุณทำงานที่ไหนคะ? Where do you work?

B: Tîi rohng pah yah bahn kráhp. Pŏhm bpehn măw.
ที่โรงพยาบาลครับ ผมเป็นหมอ At a hospital. I am a doctor.

A: Koon ah yóo tâo rai káh?[5]
คุณอายุเท่าไรคะ? How old are you?

B: Sìi sìp bpii kráhp.
สี่สิบปีครับ 40 years old.

A: Kàwp koon kàh.
ขอบคุณค่ะ Thank you.

GRAMMAR NOTES

[1] 'Bpehn' เป็น, acting like the verb 'to be', is used to indicate nationality, relationship and career. It is almost always followed by a noun. Observe the word order as follows:

Ex. Káo bpehn kohn tai.
เค้าเป็นคนไทย He/she is Thai.

Ex. Di cháhn bpehn kroo.
ดิฉันเป็นครู I am a teacher.

Ex. K<u>oo</u>n jim bp<u>e</u>hn săh mii di ch<u>á</u>hn.
    คุณจิมเป็นสามีดิฉัน Khun Jim is my husband.

2 'D<u>è</u>hk' เด็ก means a child or children in general. If you want to refer to someone's child/children, use the word 'lôok' ลูก instead.

Ex. Lôok k<u>oo</u>n ah y<u>ó</u>o tâo rai k<u>á</u>h?
    ลูกคุณอายุเท่าไรคะ? How old is your child?
Ex. D<u>è</u>hk châwp bpai rohng rian.
    เด็กชอบไปโรงเรียน Children like to go to school.

3 'Kùap' ขวบ is used as a classifier to indicate the age of a child. For adult, use the word 'bpii' ปี instead.

Ex. Lôok chah-ii p<u>ŏ</u>hm ah y<u>ó</u>o sìi kùap.
    ลูกชายผมอายุสี่ขวบ My son is 4 years old.
Ex. P<u>a</u>hn r<u>a</u>h yah p<u>ŏ</u>hm ah y<u>ó</u>o săhm sìp bpii.
    ภรรยาผมอายุสามสิบปี My wife is 30 years old.

4 When asking someone's name, follow the pattern; 'K<u>oo</u>n chêu arai?, คุณชื่ออะไร? by changing 'K<u>oo</u>n' คุณ to another pronoun.

Ex. Káo chêu arai?
    เค้าชื่ออะไร? What is his/her name?
Ex. Săh mii k<u>oo</u>n chêu arai?
    สามีคุณชื่ออะไร? What is your husband's name?

5 When asking someone's age, follow the pattern; 'K<u>oo</u>n y<u>ó</u>o tâo rai? คุณอายุเท่าไร?, by changing 'K<u>oo</u>n' คุณ to another pronoun.

Ex. Káo ah y<u>ó</u>o tâo rai?
    เค้าอายุเท่าไร? How old is he/she?
Ex. K<u>oo</u>n mâe k<u>oo</u>n ah y<u>ó</u>o tâo rai?
    คุณแม่คุณอายุเท่าไร? How old is your mother?

DRILLS

1. Practice the pattern 'Káo bp<u>eh</u>n _____' เค้าเป็น _____ *He/she is ___.* by completing the sentence using the words below.

măw	หมอ	doctor
p<u>ah</u> yah bahn	พยาบาล	nurse
kroo	ครู	teacher
n<u>áh</u>k rian	นักเรียน	student
kâh râht ch<u>ah</u> gahn	ข้าราชการ	government official

2. Practice asking someone's name by completing the following sentence using the words provided. 'A B arai?' A B อะไร? *What is A's B?*

A. Pîi chah-ii káo	พี่ชายเค้า	his older brother
B. chêu	ชื่อ	name
A. Pêuan k<u>oo</u>n	เพื่อนคุณ	your friend
B. nahm s<u>ah</u> g<u>oo</u>n	นามสกุล	last name
A. P<u>ah</u>n r<u>ah</u> yah k<u>oo</u>n	ภรรยาคุณ	your wife
B. chêu l<u>êh</u>n	ชื่อเล่น	nick name

EXERCISES

1. How do you ask the question in Thai if you want to know someone's:

   A. nickname
   B. age
   C. last name
   D. name
   E. job

F. nationality
G. country

2. How do you say the following sentences in Thai?
   A. What do you like?
   B. Where is your company?
   C. What is the name of your company?
   D. Where is your wife from?
   E. How old is your younger brother?
   F. You are Thai, aren't you?
   G. What kind of work do you do?

Westerners fear the number 13. Chinese fear the number 4 but favor 8. The lucky number for Thai people is 9. In 2003, millions of baht were paid for a car license plate number 9999. Nine is seen as lucky because the word for it sounds like the word meaning 'progress'.

In an auspicious ceremony, at which Thai people invite monks to perform rites, the number of monks must be an odd number. On the contrary, an even number of monks is to perform 'inauspicious' ceremonies such as funerals, etc.

The most commonly found interest in lucky numbers relates to gambling. Gamblers try to find anything, any incident, and interpret it numerically. They sometimes also pick digits associated with data from one's life (e.g. date, day, or even time of birth).

5. Numbers

VOCABULARY

(dtua) lêhk	(ตัว)เลข	numeral
be(r)	เบอร์	number
toh rah sàhp	โทรศัพท์	telephone
be(r) toh rah sàhp	เบอร์โทรศัพท์	telephone number
krêung	ครึ่ง	half
sŏon	ศูนย์	zero
nèung	หนึ่ง	one
sǎwng	สอง	two
sǎhm	สาม	three
sìi	สี่	four
hâh	ห้า	five
hòhk	หก	six
jèht	เจ็ด	seven
bpàet	แปด	eight
gâh-oo	เก้า	nine
sìp	สิบ	ten
sìp èht	สิบเอ็ด	eleven
sìp sǎwng	สิบสอง	twelve
sìp sǎhm	สิบสาม	thirteen
yîi sìp	ยี่สิบ	twenty
yîi sìp, èht	ยี่สิบเอ็ด	twenty-one

yîi sìp, sǎwng	ยี่สิบสอง	twenty-two
yîi sìp, sǎhm	ยี่สิบสาม	twenty-three
sǎhm sìp	สามสิบ	thirty
sǎhm sìp, èht	สามสิบเอ็ด	thirty-one
sǎhm sìp, sǎwng	สามสิบสอง	thirty-two
sìi sìp	สี่สิบ	forty
sìi sìp, èht	สี่สิบเอ็ด	forty-one
gâh·oo sìp	เก้าสิบ	ninety
nèung ráw·ii	หนึ่งร้อย	one hundred
nèung pahn	หนึ่งพัน	one thousand
nèung mèun	หนึ่งหมื่น	ten thousand
nèung sǎen	หนึ่งแสน	one hundred thousand
nèung láhn	หนึ่งล้าน	one million
bpe(r) sehn	เปอร์เซ็นต์	percent

DIALOGUE 1

A: Be(r) toh rah sàhp koon arai kráhp?
   เบอร์โทรศัพท์คุณอะไรครับ ? What is your telephone number?
B: Sǒon sǎwng sǎwng jèht bpáet bpáet gâo nèung hòhk.
   ศูนย์ สอง สอง เจ็ด แปด แปด เก้า หนึ่ง หก 02 278 8916

DIALOGUE 2

A: Tâo rai kráhp?
   เท่าไรครับ? How much?
B: Sǎwng mèun, hâh pahn bàht kàh.[1]
   สองหมื่นห้าพันบาทค่ะ 25,000 baht.

GRAMMAR NOTES

[1] When telling a price that finishes with 'ráw-ii' ร้อย, 'pahn' พัน, 'mèun' หมื่น, 'săen' แสน, Thais sometimes omit the last unit term. For example:

6,500	=	hòhk pahn, hâh (omit 'ráw-ii' ร้อย) หกพันห้า
		Theoretically, this number can also be 6,005. However, when used in commercial circumstances, the price is likely to be 6,500 instead of 6,005.
78,000	=	jèht mèun, bpàet (omit 'pahn' พัน) เจ็ดหมื่นแปด
9,620,000	=	gâh-oo láhn, hòhk săen, săwng (omit 'mèun' หมื่น) เก้าล้านหกแสนสอง

When telling a price that starts with one 'nèung' หนึ่ง, Thais sometimes leave out the initial 'one'. For example:

150	=	ráw-ii, hâh sìp ร้อยห้าสิบ
1,200	=	pahn săwng พันสอง
13,000	=	mèun săhm หมื่นสาม

An easy way to quantify something in Thai, is to break the figure into several smaller amounts. For example:

67	=	60 & 7
	=	hòhk sìp, jèht หกสิบเจ็ด
567	=	500 & 60 & 7
	=	hâh ráw-ii, hòhk sìp, jèht ห้าร้อยหกสิบเจ็ด
4,567	=	4,000 & 500 & 60 & 7
	=	sìi pahn, hâh ráw-ii, hòhk sìp, jèht สี่พันห้าร้อยหกสิบเจ็ด
34,567	=	30,000 & 4,000 & 500 & 60 & 7
	=	săhm mèun, sìi pahn, hâh ráw-ii, hòhk sìp, jèht สามหมื่นสี่พันห้าร้อยหกสิบเจ็ด

234,567 = 200,000 & 30,000 & 4,000 & 500 & 60 & 7
= sǎwng sǎen, sǎhm mèun, sìi p<u>ah</u>n, hâh ráw-ii, h<u>ò</u>hk sìp, j<u>è</u>ht
สองแสนสามหมื่นสี่พันห้าร้อยหกสิบเจ็ด

1,234,567 = 1,000,000 & 200,000 & 30,000 & 4,000 & 500 & 60 & 7
= n<u>è</u>ung láhn, sǎwng sǎen, sǎhm mèun, sìi p<u>ah</u>n, hâh ráw-ii, h<u>ò</u>hk sìp, j<u>è</u>ht
หนึ่งล้านสองแสนสามหมื่นสี่พันห้าร้อยหกสิบเจ็ด

DRILLS

1. Repeat after the audio.

   A. gâh-oo sìp   เก้าสิบ   90
   B. bpàet ráw-ii, gâh-oo sìp   แปดร้อยเก้าสิบ   890
   C. j<u>è</u>ht p<u>ah</u>n, bpàet ráw-ii, gâh-oo sìp   เจ็ดพันแปดร้อยเก้าสิบ   7,890
   D. h<u>ò</u>hk mèun, j<u>è</u>ht p<u>ah</u>n, bpàet ráw-ii, gâh-oo sìp
      หกหมื่นเจ็ดพันแปดร้อยเก้าสิบ   67,890
   E. hâh sǎen, h<u>ò</u>hk mèun, j<u>è</u>ht p<u>ah</u>n, bpàet ráw-ii, gâh-oo sìp
      ห้าแสนหกหมื่นเจ็ดพันแปดร้อยเก้าสิบ   567,890
   F. sìi láhn, hâh sǎen, h<u>ò</u>hk mèun, j<u>è</u>ht p<u>ah</u>n, bpàet ráw-ii gâh-oo sìp   สี่ล้านห้าแสนหกหมื่นเจ็ดพันแปดร้อยเก้าสิบ   4,567,890

2. Say the following amounts while omitting the last word.

   A. sǎwng p<u>ah</u>n, hâh ráw-ii   สองพันห้าร้อย   2,500
   B. sìi mèun, n<u>è</u>ung p<u>ah</u>n   สี่หมื่นหนึ่งพัน   41,000
   C. bpàet láhn, j<u>è</u>ht sǎen, sǎhm mèun
      แปดล้านเจ็ดแสนสามหมื่น   8,730,000
   D. gâh-oo sǎen, h<u>ò</u>hk mèun   เก้าแสนหกหมื่น   960,000
   E. n<u>è</u>ung p<u>ah</u>n, sǎwng ráw-ii   หนึ่งพันสองร้อย   1,200

F. bpàet láhn, sìi săen แปดล้านสี่แสน 8,400,000

EXERCISES

1. Say the following amounts in Thai.
   A. 21
   B. 167
   C. 2,790
   D. 56,987
   E. 234,085
   F. 2,130,650

2. Change the following amounts into numerals.
   A. p<u>ah</u>n sìi พันสี่
   B. săwng mèun hâh สองหมื่นห้า
   C. j<u>èh</u>t láhn, bpàet mèun เจ็ดล้านแปดหมื่น
   D. h<u>òh</u>k săen, săhm p<u>ah</u>n หกแสนสามพัน
   E. mèun h<u>òh</u>k หมื่นหก
   F. bpàet ráw·ii, yîi sìp แปดร้อยยี่สิบ

In Thailand, food is very important. It is not uncommon for Thai people to strive for good food no matter how far away the restaurant or food stall is. Thai people have a habit of eating regardless of the time of day or night. Rice is the staple in the Thai diet. That explains why the Thai phrase 'to eat rice' also means 'to eat' in general. Since rice is the staple food in Thailand, it is usually eaten at every meal. Thai cuisine is famous for its peppers and spices since most Thai dishes are cooked with basic ingredients such as garlic, chillies, lime juice, fresh coriander leaves and fermented fish sauce. Thailand's most popular soup dish is 'Tom Yum Gung' meaning spicy hot shrimp soup.

When eating out in a group, Thai people will share all dishes. Often the one of higher status (older, higher rank, richer) is the one who pays. Though 'American share' is becoming more and more accepted, it is not hard to see a scene of several people scrambling to pay the bill.

Be sure to check your bill carefully, since occasionally it may include items you subsequently cancelled, or include items you never ordered or ordered but never came. Tipping is not expected in a small food stall. In restaurants, though service charge and tax are usually included in the final bill, a decent tip for good service is certainly appreciated.

6. Eating Out

VOCABULARY

doo	ดู	to look at/watch
meh noo	เมนู	menu
rah-ii gahn	รายการ	a list of something
ao	เอา	to want, to take[1]
r<u>á</u>hp	รับ	to take, to get[2]
mii	มี	to have
châwp	ชอบ	to like
kăw..n<u>àw</u>-ii	ขอ..หน่อย	May I (have)..?[3]
nîi	นี่	this
n<u>âh</u>n	นั่น	that
..nít n<u>àw</u>-ii	นิดหน่อย	a little (bit)...[4]
mâhk	มาก	a lot, much, many, very[5]
ah hăhn	อาหาร	food
ah hăhn n<u>áe</u> n<u>ah</u>m	อาหารแนะนำ	recommended food
ah hăhn t<u>áh</u> leh	อาหารทะเล	seafood
ah hăhn wâhng	อาหารว่าง	snack, appetizer
r<u>ó</u>ht (châht)	รส (ชาติ)	taste, flavor
s<u>ò</u>ht	สด	fresh
sĭa	เสีย	bad, rotten[6]
yàhng	อย่าง	kind, type (classifier)

lăh-ii + classifier	หลาย	many
tîi	ที่	an order of ... (classifier)[7]
ìik	อีก	more, again[8]
kâh-oo	ข้าว	rice
gàhp kâh-oo	กับข้าว	food you eat with rice
náhm (bplàh-oo)	น้ำ(เปล่า)	water
náhm kăeng (bplàh-oo)	น้ำแข็ง(เปล่า)	ice
krêuang dèum	เครื่องดื่ม	beverage
kăwng wăhn	ของหวาน	dessert
tŏong	ถุง	bag
glàwng	กล่อง	box
jahn	จาน	plate
chahm	ชาม	bowl
tûay	ถ้วย	cup, small bowl
gâew	แก้ว	glass
mâw	หม้อ	pot
cháwn	ช้อน	spoon
sâwm	ส้อม	fork
mîit	มีด	knife
mái jîm fahn	ไม้จิ้มฟัน	toothpick
gràh dàht tít chôo	กระดาษทิชชู่	tissue paper
kài	ไข่	egg
néua	เนื้อ	beef
(néua) mŏo	(เนื้อ)หมู	pork

(néua) gài	(เนื้อ)ไก่	chicken
bplah	ปลา	fish
gôong	กุ้ง	shrimp
bplah mèuk	ปลาหมึก	squid
prík	พริก	chilli, pepper
pàhk	ผัก	vegetable
pŏhn lah máh-ii	ผลไม้	fruit
náhm pŏhn lah máh-ii	น้ำผลไม้	fruit juice
chah	ชา	tea
gah fae	กาแฟ	coffee
yehn	เย็น	cool
ráwn	ร้อน	hot
chah yehn	ชาเย็น	ice-tea (with milk)
gah fae yehn	กาแฟเย็น	ice-coffee
pèht	เผ็ด	hot spicy
pàht	ผัด	stir fry
tâwt	ทอด	deep fry
dtôhm	ต้ม	boil
dtŏon	ตุ๋น	stew
yâhng	ย่าง	grill
nêung	นึ่ง	steam
pí sèht	พิเศษ	special
tahm mah dah	ธรรมดา	regular, normal
ah ràw-ii	อร่อย	delicious

FOOD GUIDE

- Simple Noodle dishes

gŭay dtĭaw	ก๋วยเตี๋ยว	noodle
gŭay dtĭaw ná<u>hm</u>	ก๋วยเตี๋ยวน้ำ	noodle soup
s<u>êh</u>n l<u>éh</u>k náhm	เส้นเล็กน้ำ	small strand noodle soup
s<u>êh</u>n yài náhm	เส้นใหญ่น้ำ	big strand noodle soup
s<u>êh</u>n mìi náhm	เส้นหมี่น้ำ	thin strand noodle soup
b<u>àh</u> mìi náhm	บะหมี่น้ำ	egg noodle soup
gŭay dtĭaw hâeng	ก๋วยเตี๋ยวแห้ง	dry noodle dish
gŭay dtĭaw râht nâh	ก๋วยเตี๋ยวราดหน้า	noodle with gravy
gŭay dtĭaw p<u>àh</u>t si íw	ก๋วยเตี๋ยวผัดซีอิ๊ว	noodle with soy sauce

- Simple Rice dishes

kâh-oo dt<u>ôh</u>m bplah	ข้าวต้มปลา	rice porridge with fish
kâh-oo nâh bp<u>èh</u>t	ข้าวหน้าเป็ด	rice with duck
kâh-oo m<u>ah</u>n gài	ข้าวมันไก่	chicken with greasy rice
kâh-oo m<u>ah</u>n gài tâwt	ข้าวมันไก่ทอด	deep-fried chicken with greasy rice
kâh-oo mŏo daeng	ข้าวหมูแดง	rice with red pork and red sauce

- Starters

tâwt <u>mah</u>n bplah	ทอดมันปลา	fish-cake
bp<u>àw</u> bp<u>ía</u> tâwt	ปอเปี๊ยะทอด	deep-fried spring roll
y<u>ah</u>m w<u>óo</u>n s<u>êh</u>n	ยำวุ้นเส้น	glass noodle salad

- Soups and Curries

gaeng	แกง	curry
gaeng néua	แกงเนื้อ	beef curry
gaeng kĭao wăhn gài	แกงเขียวหวานไก่	green curry chicken

dtôhm yahm	ต้มยำ	spicy soup dish
gaeng jèut	แกงจืด	stock, clear soup dish

- Stir-fried dishes

pàht pàhk ruam	ผัดผักรวม	stir-fried mixed vegetables
gài pàht gàh prao	ไก่ผัดกะเพรา	chicken fried with basil
mŏo pàht bprîaw wăhn	หมูผัดเปรี้ยวหวาน	sweet-sour pork
gài pàht méht máh mûang	ไก่ผัดเม็ดมะม่วง	chicken fried with cashew nuts
néua pàht náhm mahn hăw-ii	เนื้อผัดน้ำมันหอย	beef oyster sauce

- Eggs

kài	ไข่	egg
kài dah-oo	ไข่ดาว	fried-egg
kài jiaw	ไข่เจียว	deep-fried omelette
kài dtôhm	ไข่ต้ม	boiled egg

- Vegetables

pàhk	ผัก	vegetables
gàh làhm bplii	กะหล่ำปลี	cabbage
prík	พริก	chilli
tùa ngâwk	ถั่วงอก	bean sprouts
dtaeng gwah	แตงกวา	cucumber
kĭng	ขิง	ginger
hèht	เห็ด	mushroom
hŭa hăwm	หัวหอม	onion
pàhk kah náh	ผักคะน้า	kale
dtôhn hăwm	ต้นหอม	spring onion
kâh-oo pôht	ข้าวโพด	corn
máh kĕua têht	มะเขือเทศ	tomato

- Fruit

pǒhn lah máh-ii	ผลไม้	fruit
fah ràhng	ฝรั่ง	guava
dtaeng moh	แตงโม	watermelon
sàhp bpah róht	สับปะรด	pineapple
chohm pôo	ชมพู่	rose-apple
áep bpê(r)n	แอบเปิ้ล	apple
glûay	กล้วย	banana
sôhm oh	ส้มโอ	pomelo
máh mûang	มะม่วง	mango
sôhm	ส้ม	orange
máh láh gaw	มะละกอ	papaya
ngáw	เงาะ	rambutan
máh nah-oo	มะนาว	lime

- Condiment

krêuang bproong	เครื่องปรุง	condiment, seasonings
náhm sôhm	น้ำส้ม	vinegar
náhm dtahn	น้ำตาล	sugar
náhm bplah	น้ำปลา	fish sauce
prík bpòhn	พริกป่น	red chili powder
prík tai	พริกไทย	white-black pepper
prík náhm bplah	พริกน้ำปลา	fish sauce with chili and lime

DIALOGUE

A: Kǎw meh noo nàw-ii kráhp.
　ขอเมนูหน่อยครับ May I have a menu, please?

B: Nîi kàh.
　นี่ค่ะ Here it is.

A: Nîi pèht réu bplàh-oo⁹ kráhp?
　นี่เผ็ดรึเปล่าครับ? Is this spicy?

B: Pèht mâhk kàh.
   เผ็ดมากค่ะ Very spicy.

A: Mii arai[10] mâi pèht mái kráhp?
   มีอะไรไม่เผ็ดมั้ยครับ? Have you anything not spicy?

B: Mii lăh-ii yàhng kàh.
   มีหลายอย่างค่ะ There are (We have) many dishes.

A: Mii ah hăhn náe nahm arai kráhp?
   มีอาหารแนะนำอะไรครับ? What are the recommended dishes (you have)?

B: Bprîaw wăhn gôong gàhp gaeng kĭaw wăhn gài kàh.
   เปรี้ยวหวานกุ้งกับแกงเขียวหวานไก่ค่ะ Sweet & Sour Shrimp and Green Curry Chicken.

A: Mii arai ìik mái kráhp?
   มีอะไรอีกมั้ยครับ? Is there anything else (you have)?

B: Mii rah-ii gahn tîi meh noo nâh săhm kàh.
   มีรายการที่เมนูหน้าสามค่ะ There is a list on page 3.

A: Yahm néua róht châht bpehn yahng ngai kráhp?
   ยำเนื้อรสชาติเป็นยังไงครับ? How does the Beef Salad taste?

B: Pèht gàhp bprîaw nít nàw-ii kàh.
   เผ็ดกับเปรี้ยวนิดหน่อยค่ะ Spicy and a little bit sour.

A: Kăw yahm néua, bprîaw wăhn gôong, gàhp gaeng kĭaw wăhn gài, láew gâw kâh-oo bplàh-oo săwng tîi kráhp.
   ขอยำเนื้อ เปรี้ยวหวานกุ้ง กับแกงเขียวหวานไก่แล้วก็ข้าวเปล่าสองที่ครับ
   May I have Spicy Beef Salad, Sweet & Sour Shrimp and Green Curry Chicken, and two plates of rice.

B: Ráhp krêuang dèum arai káh?
   รับเครื่องดื่มอะไรคะ? What would you like to drink?

A: Kăw náhm bplàh-oo nèung kùat, coke nèung kùat láew gâw, náhm kăeng bplàh-oo săwng gâew kráhp.

ขอน้ำเปล่าหนึ่งขวด โค้กหนึ่งขวด แล้วก็น้ำแข็งเปล่าสองแก้วครับ
May I have a bottle of plain water, a bottle of coke and 2 glasses of ice please?

B: Dâi kàh. Jàh ráhp arai ìik mái káh?
ได้ค่ะ จะรับอะไรอีกมั้ยคะ? OK. Would you like to take anything else?

A: Ao gŭay dtĭao sêhn léhk náhm sài tŏong, jàh ao glàhp bâhn, yâek[11] náhm sóop dtàhng hàhk náh kráhp.
เอาก๋วยเตี๋ยวเส้นเล็กน้ำใส่ถุง จะเอากลับบ้าน แยกน้ำซุปต่างหากนะครับ I want to have a small strand noodle soup in a bag to take-away. Please separate the soup (in a different bag).

B: Pí sèht rĕu tahm mah dah káh?
พิเศษหรือธรรมดาคะ? Special or regular?

A: Tahm mah dah kráhp.
ธรรมดาครับ Regular, please.

B: Dâi kàh.
ได้ค่ะ Yes, sir.

A: Chéhk bin dûay kráhp. Ráhp bàht kreh dìt mái kráhp?
เช็คบิลด้วยครับ รับบัตรเครดิตมั้ยครับ? Check, please. Do you accept credit cards?

B: Mâi ráhp kàh, ráhp dtàe nge(r)n sòht.
ไม่รับค่ะ รับแต่เงินสด No, we only accept cash.

A: Nîi kráhp, mâi dtâwng tawn.
นี่ครับ ไม่ต้องทอน Here it is. Keep the change (No need to give back).

GRAMMAR NOTES

[1] When placing an order in a restaurant or a shop, you may use the word 'ao' เอา which is less formal than 'kăw' ขอ. 'Ao'

เอา, is always followed by a noun. Use this word when you want to have something immediately. If you want to have something in the future, or wish to get something, use the word 'yàhk mii' อยากมี or 'yàhk dâi' อยากได้ + the noun you want to have or to get.

Ex. Ao coke nèung grah bpǎwng.
เอาโค้กหนึ่งกระป๋อง I want to have a can of coke.

Ex. Káo yàhk mii róht bii ehm dàhp bê(r)n yoo.
เค้าอยากมีรถบีเอ็มดับเบิ้ลยู He wants to have a BMW car.

Ex. Wahn gè(r)t koon yàhk dâi arai?
วันเกิดคุณอยากได้อะไร? What would you like to get for (your) birthday?

When approached by street vendors and you are not interested in buying their products, you may simply say 'Mâi ao kàh/kráhp' ไม่เอาค่ะ/ครับ (*I don't want it.*)

[2] 'Ráhp' รับ has several meanings. When used by a waiter or a sales person, it means to get, to want or to buy. In some situations, it means to accept.

Ex. Ráhp kǎwng wǎhn arai káh?
รับของหวานอะไรคะ? What dessert would you like to get?

Ex. Ráhp arai káh?
รับอะไรคะ? What would you like to buy? (Can I help you?)

Ex. Tîi nîi mâi ráhp nge(r)n sòht, ráhp dtàe koo bpawng.
ที่นี่ไม่รับเงินสด รับแต่คูปอง Here, we don't accept cash but only coupons.

[3] When asking for something or to do something, say 'kǎw' ขอ (*May I have...?*) You may soften the request by adding 'nàw-ii' หน่อย or 'nàw-ii dâi mái?' หน่อยได้มั้ย? at the end of the sentence.

Ex. Kăw chah m<u>a</u>h nah-oo nàw-ii kr<u>á</u>hp.
ขอชามะนาวหน่อยครับ May I have lemon-tea please?

Ex. Kăw chái toh r<u>a</u>h sàhp nàw-ii dâi mái kr<u>á</u>hp.
ขอใช้โทรศัพท์หน่อยได้มั้ยครับ? Could I use the phone please?

4·5 '..nít nàw-ii' นิดหน่อย means 'a little (bit)...' and '..mâhk' มาก means a lot, very. Both come after the verb, adverb or adjective they modify.

Ex. P<u>ŏ</u>hm châwp rohng raem níi nít nàw-ii.
ผมชอบโรงแรมนี้นิดหน่อย I like this hotel a little bit.

Or P<u>ŏ</u>hm châwp rohng raem níi mâhk.
ผมชอบโรงแรมนี้มาก I like this hotel a lot.

Ex. Wăhn nít nàw-ii.
หวานนิดหน่อย A little bit sweet.

Or Wăhn mâhk.
หวานมาก Very sweet.

Ex. Cháh nít nàw-ii.
ช้านิดหน่อย A little bit slow.

Or Cháh mâhk.
ช้ามาก Very slow.

6 'Sĭa' เสีย means bad, rotten and also out-of-order, broken, not working. Thus, you can use this word for food, equipment, appliances, and so forth. The word 'láew' แล้ว (*already*) may be added at the end of the sentence.

Ex. Ae sĭa.
แอร์เสีย The air-conditioner is broken.

Ex. Bpàhk gah sĭa láew.
ปากกาเสียแล้ว The pen is broken already.

Ex. P<u>ŏ</u>hn l<u>a</u>h máh-ii níi sĭa láew.
ผลไม้นี่เสียแล้ว This fruit is rotten already.

7 When ordering food or beverage, if you do not remember its classifier, you may opt for the word 'tîi' ที่ instead. 'Tîi' ที่, in this context means 'serving'. The classifier is positioned after the amount it quantifies. More details of this subject are explained in the 'Shopping' topic.

    Ex. Kăw gài tâwt nèung tîi gàhp gah fae yehn nèung tîi.
           ขอไก่ทอดหนึ่งที่กับกาแฟเย็นหนึ่งที่ May I have one serving of deep-fried chicken and one ice-coffee?

8 'Ìik' อีก means more, again. It is usually placed after verb or object (noun), if any.

    Ex. Mii bia ìik mái kráhp?
           มีเบียร์อีกมั้ยครับ? Do you have more beer?

    Ex. Mii ìik sìi kùat kráhp.
           มีอีกสี่ขวดครับ (I) have four more bottles.

    Ex. Pŏhm mii gah fae ìik nèung tûay, koon jàh dèum mái?
           ผมมีกาแฟอีกหนึ่งถ้วย คุณจะดื่มมั้ย? I have one more cup of coffee. Do you want to drink it?

    Ex. Ao ìik nàw-ii kráhp.
           เอาอีกหน่อยครับ (I) want a little bit more please.

    Ex. Koon măw yàhk dtrùat koon ìik kráhng kàh.
           คุณหมออยากตรวจคุณอีกครั้งค่ะ The doctor wants to examine you one more time.

9 Réu bplàh-oo?' รึเปล่า? is a question word that appears at the end of the sentence. It literally means 'or not?' To answer 'Yes' to this kind of question, just repeat the key word. To answer 'No', just say 'bplàh-oo' เปล่า or 'mâi ไม่ + key word'.

    Ex. Koon hĭw réu bplàh-oo káh?
           คุณหิวรึเปล่าคะ? Are you hungry?

Yes: Hĭw káh.
   หิวค่ะ Yes, I am hungry.
No: Bplàh-oo / mâi hĭw kàh.
   เปล่า/ไม่หิวค่ะ No, I am not hungry.

[10] 'Arai' อะไร, if not functioning as a question word, means 'anything'. The same rule applies to some other question words including 'tîi năi' ที่ไหน (*anywhere*) and 'krai' ใคร (*anybody*).

Ex. Mii arai mâi pèht pèht mái kráhp?
   มีอะไรเผ็ดๆ มั้ยครับ? Have you anything spicy?
Ex. Mii arai ìik mái kráhp?
   มีอะไรอีกมั้ยครับ? Is there anything else?

[11] 'Yâek แยก+ noun, mean 'to separate...' To separate one thing from another thing, the word 'dtàhng hàhk' ต่างหาก may be added after the noun.

Ex. Yâek bin.
   แยกบิล To separate the bill.
Ex. Yâek náhm jîm dtàhng hàhk.
   แยกน้ำจิ้มต่างหาก To separate sauce (from a dish).

DRILLS

1. Practice 'Nîi___réu bplàh-oo? นี่___รึเปล่า? *Is this___?* by completing the sentence using the following words.

ah ràw-ii	อร่อย	delicious
sài choo róht	ใส่ชูรส	put MSG
ráwn	ร้อน	hot
yehn	เย็น	cool/cold
sàh àht	สะอาด	clean
sòhk gah bpròhk	สกปรก	dirty

| sòok | สุก | ripe, well done |
| dìp | ดิบ | raw |

2. Practice 'Mii arai mâi__mái? มีอะไรไม่__มั้ย? *Is there anything not____?* by completing the sentence using the following words.

p<u>è</u>ht	เผ็ด	spicy
wăhn	หวาน	sweet
bprîaw	เปรี้ยว	sour
k<u>e</u>hm	เค็ม	salty
m<u>a</u>hn	มัน	oily
jèut	จืด	bland
k<u>ŏ</u>hm	ขม	bitter

3. Practice 'Kăw___nàw·ii'. ขอ__หน่อย *May I (have)__ please?* by completing the sentence using the following words.

s<u>à</u>hng ah hăhn	สั่งอาหาร	order food
n<u>â</u>hng	นั่ง	sit
doo	ดู	watch, look
lawng	ลอง	try out
chim	ชิม	taste (v.)
f<u>a</u>hng	ฟัง	listen
àhn	อ่าน	read
kâh·oo p<u>à</u>ht	ข้าวผัด	fried-rice

EXERCISES

1. Find an English equivalent.

   A. Kăw kâh·oo ìik k<u>à</u>h.
   ขอข้าวอีกค่ะ

B. Pŏhn lah mái nîi sĭa láew kàh.
ผลไม้นี่เสียแล้วค่ะ

C. Mii náhm kăeng ìik mái kráhp?
มีน้ำแข็งอีกมั้ยครับ?

D. Kăw chah ìik săhm tûay kráhp.
ขอชาอีกสามถ้วยครับ

E. Mâi sài pŏhng choo róht kàh.
ไม่ใส่ผงชูรสค่ะ

F. Ráhp krêuang dèum arai dii káh?
รับเครื่องดื่มอะไรดีคะ?

G. Sài prík nít nàw-ii kráhp.
ใส่พริกนิดหร่อยครับ

H. Ao sòok mâhk mâhk kráhp.
เอาสุกมากๆ ครับ

I. Tîi nîi arai ah ràw-ii kráhp.
ที่นี่อะไรอร่อยครับ?

2. Find a Thai equivalent.
   A. Could I have three more ice-coffee please?
   B. I would like to have fried-rice for take-away please.
   C. Check! Please.
   D. Keep the change.
   E. I didn't order this dish.
   F. I want it very spicy.
   G. Please separate the bills.
   H. May I have the menu, please?
   I. Very delicious.

Bargaining is like a game. In keeping with the spirit of the game, negotiations should be carried out in a good-humored manner. The seller expects that the buyer will offer a lower price than asked. The buyer believes that the seller will first offer an 'over-price'. Sometimes buyers may leave the shop, only to be called back and negotiations would continue.

References may be made to a previous purchase or to cheaper prices offered by other shops. You should try to get some idea of what a reasonable price is prior to beginning a negotiation. You may look around and compare the prices or observe others negotiate before attempting to bargain down the price.

Telling the shopkeeper in Thai that you live in Thailand might help you get a better price.

7. Shopping

VOCABULARY

séu	ซื้อ	to buy
kăwng	ของ	things
kăwng lêhn	ของเล่น	toy
mii	มี	to have, to be in 'existence'
mòht	หมด	to be finished, out of stock[1]
séu kăwng	ซื้อของ	to do shopping
kăh-ii	ขาย	to sell
lawng	ลอง	to try out
sài	ใส่	to put on, to wear
gàhp	กับ	and, with[2]
láew gâw	แล้วก็	and, and then[3]
dûay	ด้วย	too, as well
tîi	ที่	at
tîi năi	ที่ไหน?	where?
mêua rai?	เมื่อไร?	when?
rah kah	ราคา	price
lóht (rah kah)	ลด(ราคา)	to discount
gìi + (classifier)?	กี่	how many...?[4]
lăh-ii + (classifier)	หลาย	many...[5]
(classifier) + năi?	ไหน?	which...?
tâo rai?	เท่าไร?	how much?
yàhk dâi + something	อยากได้	to want to have something[6]

yàhk + verb	อยาก	to want to do something[7]
yàhk hâi + someone + verb	อยากให้	to want someone to do something[8]
ao + something	เอา +	to want something[9]
..dâi	ได้	to be able to[10]
gào	เก่า	old (thing)
gàe	แก่	old (person)
mài	ใหม่	new
... + gwàh	กว่า	more + ...[11]
... + tîi s<u>òo</u>t	ที่สุด	the most + ...[12]
...+ ge(r)n bpai	เกินไป	too (much) + ...[13]
t<u>óo</u>k yàhng	ทุกอย่าง	everything[14]
bahng yàhng	บางอย่าง	something[15]
k<u>a</u>h nàht	ขนาด	size
sái	ไซส์	size
l<u>é</u>hk	เล็ก	small
glahng	กลาง	medium
yài	ใหญ่	big
yah-oo	ยาว	long
s<u>â</u>hn	สั้น	short
k<u>á</u>hp	คับ	tight
paw dii	พอดี	fit well
sǐi	สี	color
kǎh-oo	ขาว	white
d<u>a</u>hm	ดำ	black

daeng	แดง	red
kĭaw	เขียว	green
lĕuang	เหลือง	yellow
sôhm	ส้ม	orange
náhm dtahn	น้ำตาล	brown
náhm nge(r)n	น้ำเงิน	blue
chohm poo	ชมพู	pink
tao	เทา	gray
(color) + àwn	อ่อน	light color
(color) + kêhm	เข้ม	dark color
sêua pâh	เสื้อผ้า	clothes
sêua pâh pôo yĭng	เสื้อผ้าผู้หญิง	women's clothes
sêua pâh pôo chah-ii	เสื้อผ้าผู้ชาย	men's clothes
sêua pâh dèhk	เสื้อผ้าเด็ก	children's clothes
sêua	เสื้อ	shirt
sêua yêut	เสื้อยืด	T-shirt
sêua kăen sâhn	เสื้อแขนสั้น	short-sleeved shirt
sêua kăen yah-oo	เสื้อแขนยาว	long-sleeved shirt
gahng gehng	กางเกง	trousers, pants
gahng gehng kăh sâhn	กางเกงขาสั้น	shorts
gahng gehng kăh yah-oo	กางเกงขายาว	trousers
gràh bprohng	กระโปรง	skirt
gràh bprohng sâhn	กระโปรงสั้น	short skirt
gràh bprohng yah-oo	กระโปรงยาว	long skirt

krêuang chái	เครื่องใช้	appliance
bpàhk gah	ปากกา	pen
gr<u>à</u>h dàht	กระดาษ	paper
n<u>ă</u>hng sěu	หนังสือ	book
n<u>ă</u>hng sěu pim	หนังสือพิมพ์	newspaper
t<u>ŏo</u>ng	ถุง	paper/plastic bag
glâwng	กล้อง	camera
krêuang chái fai fáh	เครื่องใช้ไฟฟ้า	electric appliance
ae	แอร์	air-conditioner
p<u>á</u>ht l<u>oh</u>m	พัดลม	fan
tii wii	ทีวี	TV
wít t<u>ah</u> yóo	วิทยุ	radio
toh r<u>ah</u> s<u>àh</u>p	โทรศัพท์	telephone

DIALOGUE

A: S<u>àh</u> w<u>àh</u>t dii k<u>àh</u>. J<u>àh</u> r<u>áh</u>p arai dii k<u>áh</u>?
สวัสดีค่ะ จะรับอะไรดีคะ? Hello. What would you like to have?

B: Sêua yêut, kăen s<u>âh</u>n, sǐi d<u>ah</u>m, sái L, mii mái kr<u>áh</u>p?
เสื้อยืดแขนสั้นสีดำไซส์แอล มีมั้ยครับ? Do you have an L size, short-sleeved shirt, in black?

A: Sǐi d<u>ah</u>m, sái L, m<u>òh</u>t k<u>àh</u>.
สีดำไซส์แอลหมดค่ะ We ran out of the L size in black.

B: Mêua rai j<u>àh</u> mii ìik kr<u>áh</u>p?
เมื่อไรจะมีอีกครับ? When will you have it again?

A: Y<u>ah</u>ng mâi s<u>âh</u>p[16] k<u>àh</u>. Sǐi kǎh-oo dâi mái k<u>áh</u>?
ยังไม่ทราบค่ะ สีขาวได้มั้ยคะ? I don't know yet. Is white color OK?

B: Mâi ao sĭi kăh-oo kráhp. Sĭi daeng, mii sái arai kráhp?
ไม่เอาสีขาวครับ สีแดงมีไซส์อะไรครับ? I don't want white. What sizes do you have in red?

A: Mii sái S gàhp M kàh.
มีไซส์เอสกับเอ็มค่ะ We have S and M.

B: Kăw lawng nàw-ii dâi mái kráhp?
ขอลองหน่อยได้มั้ยครับ? May I try it on please?

A: Dâi kàh. Hâwng lawng yòo tîi nâhn kàh.
ได้ค่ะ ห้องลองอยู่ที่นั่นค่ะ Yes. The fitting rooms are there.

☙ ☙ ☙

A: Paw dii mái káh?
พอดีมั้ยคะ? Does it fit well?

B: Léhk ge(r)n bpai kráhp. Yài gwàh níi, mii mái kráhp?
เล็กเกินไปครับ ใหญ่กว่านี้มีมั้ยครับ? It's too small. Do you have a bigger one?

A: Mii sái XL, yài tîi sòot kàh.
มีไซส์เอ็กซ์แอลใหญ่ที่สุดค่ะ Yes, we have XL, the biggest size.

B: Ao sĭi daeng gàhp sĭi kĭao kêhm, sái XL kráhp. Umm...bàep náhn mii sĭi sôhm dûay mái kráhp?
เอาสีแดงกับสีเขียวเข้มไซส์เอ็กซ์แอลครับ อืม...แบบนั้นมีสีส้มด้วย มั้ยครับ? I want XL in red and in dark green. Umm...do you also have that style in orange?

A: Bàep năi káh?
แบบไหนคะ? Which style?

B: Bàep náhn kráhp.
แบบนั้นครับ That style!

A: Mii kàh. Jàh ráhp gìi dtua káh?
มีค่ะ จะรับกี่ตัวคะ? Yes, I have. How many would you like?

B: Ao nèung dtua kráhp. Dtua láh[17] tâo rai kráhp?
เอาหนึ่งตัวครับ ตัวละเท่าไรครับ? I'll take one (orange color). How much is one (shirt)?

A: Dtua láh săhm ráw-ii bàht kàh.
ตัวละสามร้อยบาทค่ะ Three hundred baht each.

B: Táhng mòht tâo rai kráhp?
ทั้งหมดเท่าไรครับ? How much is it in total?

A: Gâo-oo ráw-ii bàht kàh.
เก้าร้อยบาทค่ะ Nine hundred baht.

B: Lòht dâi mái kráhp? Pŏhm séu lăh-ii dtua.
ลดได้มั้ยครับ? ผมซื้อหลายตัว Can you give discount? I bought many shirts.

A: Lòht dâi nít nàw-ii kàh.
ลดได้นิดหน่อยค่ะ I can give you a little bit discount.

B: Bpàet ráw-ii bàht dâi mái kráhp?
แปดร้อยบาทได้มั้ยครับ? Eight hundred baht can do?

A: Dâi kàh.
ได้ค่ะ OK.

B: Kăw tôht kráhp, pŏhm jàh séu bpàhk gah dâi tîi năi kráhp?
ขอโทษครับ ผมจะซื้อปากกาได้ที่ไหนครับ? Excuse me, where can I buy a pen?

A: Tîi cháhn hâh kàh.
ที่ชั้นห้าค่ะ On the fifth floor.

GRAMMAR NOTES

[1] 'mòht' หมด is used behind a noun and may be followed by 'láew' แล้ว (*already*). It indicates something is 'used up', 'exhausted' or 'out of stock'.

Ex. Gin kâh-oo mòht láew kàh.

Ex. Náhm dtahn mòht láew kàh.
กินข้าวหมดแล้วค่ะ I already finished my food. (nothing left)
น้ำตาลหมดแล้วค่ะ The sugar is out of stock.

In the case of finishing an activity, use 'sèht' เสร็จ after the verb it modifies.
Ex. Tahm ngahn sèht láew kàh.
ทำงานเสร็จแล้วค่ะ I finished my work already.

2-3 'gàhp' กับ is used for connecting noun with noun while 'láew gâw' แล้วก็ is used for connecting noun with noun, or, phrase with phrase, or, sentence with sentence.
Ex. Dì cháhn châwp chah, gàhp gah fae, tîi nîi.
ดิฉันชอบชากับกาแฟที่นี่ I like the tea and coffee here.
Ex. Pŏhm jàh bpai hăh măw, láew gâw, jàh glàhp bâhn.
ผมจะไปหาหมอแล้วก็จะกลับบ้าน I am going to see the doctor and then return home.

4-5 Apply a 'classifier' when you want to quantify nouns. Classifiers are words used to specify the unit used in counting or referring to them. (e.g. a piece of paper, a cup of tea, a bottle of water) A group of nouns that have some features in common share the same classifier.

Classifiers are also used with the singular form of the noun where an individual thing is specially referred to. When the noun is qualified by the adjectives 'diaw' เดียว (*single/one*), 'râek' แรก (*first*), 'nâh' หน้า (*front*), 'lăhng' หลัง (*behind*), 'sòot táh-ii' สุดท้าย (*last*), or ordinal numbers, these words come after the classifier.
Ex. Róht kahn níi dii mâhk.
รถคันนี้ดีมาก This car is very good.
Ex. Di cháhn mii bâhn lăhng diaw (tâo náhn).
ดิฉันมีบ้านหลังเดียว (เท่านั้น) I have one house (only).

Ex. Róht meh kahn sòot táh-ii àwk gìi mohng káh?
รถเมล์คันสุดท้ายออกกี่โมงคะ? What time does the last bus leave?

When a noun is qualified by the adjectives; 'pûak níi' พวกนี้ (*these*), 'pûak náhn' พวกนั้น (*those*), 'mâhk' มาก (*a lot*), 'náw-ii' น้อย (*a little bit*), a classifier is not used.

Ex. Dèhk pûak níi sohn jing jing.
เด็กพวกนี้ซนจริงๆ These children are really naughty.

Once having established the noun referred to, it is usual to omit it in subsequent conversation and use only the classifier. In a large number of cases where there is no suitable classifier, the noun itself is repeated and used as its own classifier. In this case the classifier is usually omitted when the noun is in the singular form.

GROUP	CLASSIFIER	
People	kohn	คน
Animals, tables, chairs, shirts, trousers, clothes	dtua	ตัว
Houses, buildings	lǎhng	หลัง
Cars, land vehicles	kahn	คัน
Shoes, socks, anything in pairs	kôo	คู่
Cups, glasses, plates, hats, bags	bai	ใบ
Balls, melons, anything in a round shape	lôok	ลูก
Papers, anything in a flat thin shape	pàen	แผ่น
TV, computer, electronic appliances	krêuang	เครื่อง
Any small items	ahn	อัน
Books	lêhm	เล่ม

Apply this pattern when referring to quantity:
Noun + Number + Classifier

To inquire about an amount of something, simply replace the number with the word 'gìi' กี่.

Ex. D<u>tóh</u> săwng dtua.
โต๊ะสองตัว Two tables.

Ex. Bâhn sìi l<u>ăh</u>ng
บ้านสี่หลัง Four houses.

Ex. Tîi nîi mii k<u>oh</u>n Thai lăh-ii k<u>oh</u>n.
ที่นี่มีคนไทยหลายคน There are many Thais here.

Ex. Tîi nîi mii k<u>oh</u>n Thai gìi k<u>oh</u>n?
ที่นี่มีคนไทยกี่คน? How many Thais are there here?

6–8 There are several Thai words meaning 'to want'. These are:
'yàhk dâi' อยากได้ + something = to wish for possession of
Ex. Káo yàhk dâi r<u>óh</u>t.
เค้าอยากได้รถ She/he wants to have a car.

yàhk อยาก + verb = to want to do something
Ex. Káo yàhk bpai Pattaya.
เค้าอยากไปพัทยา She/he wants to go to Pattaya.

yàhk hâi อยากให้ + someone + to do something = to want someone to do somehing
Ex. Káo yàhk hâi k<u>oo</u>n bpai hăh.
เค้าอยากให้คุณไปหา She/he wants you to visit (go and see) him/her.

9 ao เอา + something = to want to get something, used for an immediate action and for buying things, ordering food, etc.
Ex. Ao náhm săwng kùat k<u>àh</u>.
เอาน้ำสองขวดค่ะ I want two bottles of water.

Ex. Mâi ao sĭi kăh-oo, ao sĭi d<u>ah</u>m.
ไม่เอาสีขาว เอาสีดำ I don't want white, I want black.

[10] 'Dâi' ได้ has many meanings. When placed at the end of a sentence, it means 'can'. To make it negative, put 'mâi' ไม่ in front of dâi ได้. Thus 'mâi dâi' ไม่ได้ that appears at the end of the sentence means 'can't'.
However, when 'mâi dâi' ไม่ได้ is put in front of a verb, it means 'didn't'. When 'dâi' ได้ is used in response to a request or order, it means 'Yes'.

Ex. P<u>ŏh</u>m pôot pah săh tai mâi dâi kr<u>áh</u>p.
ผมพูดภาษาไทยไม่ได้ครับ I can't speak Thai.

Ex. P<u>ŏh</u>m mâi dâi pôot pah săh tai kr<u>áh</u>p.
ผมไม่ได้พูดภาษาไทยครับ I didn't speak Thai.

To 'know how' to do something, you may say 'bp<u>eh</u>n' เป็น instead of 'dâi' ได้.

Ex. P<u>ŏh</u>m pôot pah săh tai bp<u>eh</u>n kr<u>áh</u>p.
ผมพูดภาษาไทยเป็นครับ I can speak Thai.

[11-12] Put 'gwàh' กว่า behind an adjective or adverb to make a comparative expression. Put 'tîi s<u>òo</u>t' ที่สุด to make a superlative expression.

Ex. Dt<u>óh</u> dtua níi n<u>àh</u>k gwàh dtua n<u>áh</u>n.
โต๊ะตัวนี้หนักกว่าตัวนั้น This table is heavier than that table.

Ex. <u>Ah</u> meh ri gah yài gwàh sĭng <u>kah</u> bpoh.
อเมริกาใหญ่กว่าสิงคโปร์ America is bigger than Singapore.

Ex. Jim sŏong tîi s<u>òo</u>t nai bâhn.
จิมสูงที่สุดในบ้าน Jim is the tallest in the house.

Ex. Ráhn níi dii tîi s<u>òo</u>t.
ร้านนี้ดีที่สุด This shop is the best.

[13] '...+ ge(r)n bpai' เกินไป = too much ...

Ex. Kăwng tîi nîi paeng ge(r)n bpai.
ของที่นี่แพงเกินไป Things here are too expensive.

Ex. Ah hăhn nîi pèht ge(r)n bpai
อาหารนี่เผ็ดเกินไป This food is too spicy.

14 'tóok yàhng' ทุกอย่าง (*everything*), 'tóok' ทุก itself means 'every' and 'yàhng' อย่าง is equivalent to 'kind', 'type', mostly used as a classifier. There are several Thai words compounded with 'tóok' ทุก, namely 'tóok wahn' ทุกวัน (*everyday*), 'tóok tîi' ทุกที่ (*everywhere*), 'tóok kohn' ทุกคน (*everyone*), etc.

15 'bahng yàhng' บางอย่าง (*something*), 'bahng' บาง itself means 'some'. There are several Thai words compounded with 'bahng' บาง, namely 'bahng bpii' บางปี (*some years*), "bahng tîi" บางที่ (*some places*), 'bahng kohn' บางคน (*some people*), 'bahng kráhng' บางครั้ง (*sometimes*).

16 'sâhp' ทราบ or 'róo' รู้ means to know a fact but 'sâhp' ทราบ is more formal. In many constructions they are interchangeable but not in all. 'Róo jàhk' รู้จัก means to be acquainted with a person, thing or place.

17 When asking the price per unit, say:
'Noun + (rah kah ราคา) + Classifier + láh tâo rai ละเท่าไร?'
Ex. Rawng táo (rah kah) kôo láh tâo rai?'
รองเท้า (ราคา) คู่ละเท่าไร? How much is a pair of shoes?

If you are not sure how the merchandise is sold, (i.e. per item or per kilo, etc), you may ask:
'Nîi kăh-ii yahng ngai?' นี่ขายยังไง? = How do you sell this?
Ex. Pŏhn lah mái nîi kăh-ii yahng ngai?'
ผลไม้นี่ขายยังไง? How do you sell this fruit?

When asking the price of a particular item, say:
Noun + (rah kah ราคา) + Classifier + níi นี้ (this) / náhn นั้น (that) tâo rai เท่าไร?

Ex. Sêua dtua níi (rah kah) tâo rai?
เสื้อตัวนี้ (ราคา) เท่าไร? How much is this shirt?

Ex. Nǎhng sěu lêhm náhn (rah kah) tâo rai?
หนังสือเล่มนั้น (ราคา) เท่าไร? How much is that book?

DRILLS

1. Practice ' *Noun* + nîi นี่ + *classifier* + láh tâo rai? ละเท่าไร?' *How much is this noun per unit* ? by replacing the italicized words with the following.

Noun			Classifier	
kěhm kàht	เข็มขัด	belt	sěhn	เส้น
mùak	หมวก	hat	bai	ใบ
rawng táh-oo	รองเท้า	shoe	kôo	คู่
tǒong táh-oo	ถุงเท้า	sock	kôo	คู่
gràh bpǎo	กระเป๋า	handbag	bai	ใบ
krêuang meu	เครื่องมือ	tool	ahn	อัน

2. Practice 'Noun + classifier + nǎi? ไหน?' *Which one?* by replacing the italicized words with those in the following list.
Note: Some nouns are also classifiers in their own right. In those cases, use the word just once.

Noun			Classifier	
wít tah yóo	วิทยุ	radio	krêuang	เครื่อง
wǐi	หวี	comb	ahn	อัน
maw dte(r) sai	มอเตอร์ไซด์	motorcycle	kahn	คัน
náhm	น้ำ	water	kùat	ขวด
gràh dàht	กระดาษ	paper	pàen	แผ่น
dèhk	เด็ก	child	kohn	คน
hâwng	ห้อง	room	hâwng	ห้อง

EXERCISES

1. How do you say the following sentences in Thai?
    - A: Do you have red color?
    - B: Did you empty your plate?
    - C: Are you finished?
    - D: I want to have a house.
    - E: I want to play piano.
    - F: It's too small.
    - G: Do you have a shorter one?
    - H: This is the smallest one.
    - I: I know somebody here.
    - J: How much is this pair of socks?

2. Follow the instructions.
    - A: Ask for a bottle of water and a cup of tea.
    - B: Ask how much a T-shirt is.
    - C: Ask someone if he has finished his plate.
    - D: Compare the US, Thailand and Singapore by using 'yài' ใหญ่, 'léhk' เล็ก, 'gwàh' กว่า and 'tîi sòot' ที่สุด.
    - E: Compare the price of food in the US and in Thailand.
    - F: You are trying on a shirt but it is too small. Ask if there is a bigger one.
    - G: Ask if there are other colors.
    - H: Ask if the price is negotiable.
    - I: Ask someone where you can buy a newspaper.
    - J: Ask how many people there are in this building.

When providing directions or describing a location, a Thai is apt to use the name of landmarks such as a monument, a bridge, or a building as a reference. Rather than telling the address of the destination, a Thai providing directions may say that the place is next to the Elephant Building. Thais do not give directions North, South, East and West. Instead, they may say 'walk towards the park.' When referring to a highway, Thais call them by names rather than by road numbers.

When taking a taxi, tell the driver your destination before getting in and make sure the driver turns on the meter. Tuk-tuk fare is negotiable (a tuk-tuk is a three-wheel open air vehicle, also called a "samlor"). Motorcycle taxis are popular for short distances, especially for travelling down a 'soi' (side street or lane). For long distances, the motorcycle taxi may be more expensive than a regular taxi. If you plan to go by tuk-tuk (samlor) or motorcycle taxi, check that the driver knows the location first and then agree on the fare before stepping into – or onto – the vehicle. Tipping is not necessary.

8. Directions

VOCABULARY

tahng	ทาง	way, road
sêhn tahng	เส้นทาง	route
tahng năi?	ทางไหน?	which way?
dtrohng bpai	ตรงไป	to go straight
líaw sáh-ii	เลี้ยวซ้าย	to turn left
líaw kwăh	เลี้ยวขวา	to turn right
chít sáh-ii	ชิดซ้าย	to go to/stay on the left lane
chít kwăh	ชิดขวา	to go to/stay on the right lane
yòo lehn glahng	อยู่เลนกลาง	to stay in the middle lane
tahng kwăh (meu)	ทางขวามือ	on the right (hand) side
tahng sáh-ii (meu)	ทางซ้ายมือ	on the left (hand) side
dtìt gàhp	ติดกับ	next to
yòot	หยุด	to stop
jàwt	จอด	to park, to stop a car
tăw-ii lăhng	ถอยหลัง	to reverse
glàhp róht	กลับรถ	to u-turn
kàhp róht	ขับรถ	to drive
pàhn	ผ่าน	to pass[1]
kàhp (róht) pàhn	ขับรถผ่าน	to drive past
de(r)n	เดิน	to walk
kâhm	ข้าม	to cross[2]
bpai	ไป	to go[3]
mah	มา	to come

glàhp	กลับ	to return (to a place)
tĕung	ถึง	to arrive, to reach
cháh	ช้า	slow
cháh cháh	ช้าๆ	slower (request)
reh-oo	เร็ว	fast
reh-oo reh-oo	เร็วๆ	faster (request)
fai daeng	ไฟแดง	red traffic right, traffic light
fai kĭaw	ไฟเขียว	green traffic light
săhn yahn fai	สัญญาณไฟ	traffic light
tàh nŏhn	ถนน	road
sàh pahn	สะพาน	bridge
sàh pahn law-ii	สะพานลอย	pedestrian bridge
tahng dùan	ทางด่วน	expressway
tahng yâek	ทางแยก	intersection
saw-ii	ซอย	Soi, sub-road
bpàhk saw-ii	ปากซอย	the beginning of a Soi
sòot saw-ii	สุดซอย	the end of a Soi
saw-ii dtahn	ซอยตัน	dead-end Soi
léuk	ลึก	deep
(kâhng) dtâi	(ข้าง)ใต้	under
râwp râwp	รอบๆ	around, surround
tîi hŭa moom	ที่หัวมุม	at the corner
cháhn	ชั้น	floor
bahn dai	บันได	ladder, stairs
bahn dai lêuan	บันไดเลื่อน	escalator
kêun	ขึ้น	to go up, to get on a vehicle[4]
lohng	ลง	to go down, to get off[5] a vehicle

róht	รถ	car
róht fai	รถไฟ	train
róht fai fáh	รถไฟฟ้า	sky-train, electric train
róht meh	รถเมล์	public bus
maw dte(r) sai	มอเตอร์ไซด์	motorcycle
jàhk gràh yahn	จักรยาน	bicycle
sàh tăh nii	สถานี	station
bpâh-ii róht meh	ป้ายรถเมล์	bus stop

DIALOGUE 1

A: Kăw tôht kàh, hâwng náhm yòo tîi năi káh?
ขอโทษค่ะ ห้องน้ำอยู่ที่ไหนคะ? Excuse me, where is the restroom?

B: Yòo cháhn săwng⁶, dtìt gàhp ráhn ah hăhn kráhp.
อยู่ชั้นสอง ติดกับร้านอาหารครับ It's on the second floor, next to a restaurant.

A: Bpai tahng năi káh?
ไปทางไหนคะ? Which way?

B: De(r)n dtrohng bpai, láew líaw sáh-ii, kêun bahn dai bpai. Hâwng náhm yòo tahng kwăh meu kráhp.
เดินตรงไป แล้วเลี้ยวซ้ายขึ้นบันไดไป ห้องน้ำอยู่ทางขวามือครับ Walk straight, then turn left and go upstairs. The restroom is on the right-hand side.

DIALOGUE 2

A: Kăw tôht kráhp. jàh dtòo jàhk bpai yahng ngai kráhp?
ขอโทษครับ จตุจักรไปยังไงครับ? Excuse me, how to go to Jatujak market?

B: Khêun róht fai fáh bpai lohng tîi sàh tăh-nii măw chít kàh.
ขึ้นรถไฟฟ้าไปลงที่สถานีหมอชิตค่ะ Take the sky-train and get off at Mor-chit station.

A: Khêun róht fai fáh dâi tîi năi kráhp?
ขึ้นรถไฟฟ้าได้ที่ไหนครับ? Where can I get on the sky-train?

B: De(r)n dtrohng bpai, láew líaw sáh-ii, sàh tăh nii yòo kâhng nâh kàh.
เดินตรงไป แล้วเลี้ยวซ้าย สถานีอยู่ข้างหน้าค่ะ
Walk straight, then turn left. The station is right ahead.

A: Kàwp koon kráhp.
ขอบคุณครับ Thank you.

DIALOGUE 3

A: Bpai sòo kŏom wít saw-ii sìp jèht kàh.
ไปสุขุมวิทซอยสิบเจ็ดค่ะ To Sukhumvit Soi 17, please.

B: Kâo saw-ii léuk mái kráhp?
เข้าซอยลึกมั้ยครับ? Is it (the destination) far down the Soi?

A: Mâi léuk kàh. Bpai kâe bpàhk saw-ii kàh.... Chûay kàhp reh-oo reh-oo nàw-ii dâi mái káh?
ไม่ลึกค่ะ ไปแค่ปากซอยค่ะ....ช่วยขับเร็วๆ หน่อยได้มั้ยคะ? No, just at the entrance of the Soi. Could you drive faster please?

B: Dâi kráhp....Bpai tahng dùan mái kráhp?
ได้ครับ....ไปทางด่วนมั้ยครับ? Yes....Do you want to take the expressway?

A: Mâi dtâwng kàh, bpai tahng tàh nŏhn péht chah boo rii kàh.
ไม่ต้องค่ะ ไปทางถนนเพชรบุรีค่ะ No need, take Petchburi road.

GRAMMAR NOTES

1. You can use the word 'pàhn' ผ่าน (*to pass*) as a verb or as an adverb. (*past*)

    Ex. Taxi pê(r)ng jàh pàhn bpai.
    แท็กซี่เพิ่งจะผ่านไป A taxi just passed by.

    Ex. Mêua wahn níi pŏhm de(r)n pàhn dtàh làht .
    เมื่อวานนี้ผม เดินผ่านตลาด Yesterday I walked past the market.

    If your taxi driver accidentally passes your destination, say: pàhn mah láew ผ่านมาแล้ว or le(r)-ii mah láew. เลยมาแล้ว

2-3. Verbs concerning motion (e.g. to cross, to drive, to walk, to run, to call, to pass, etc) are usually used in combination with 'bpai' ไป or 'mah' มา. These two words indicate the direction of motion relative to the speaker; 'bpai' ไป means away from the speaker and 'mah' มา means toward the speaker.

    Ex. Pŏhm kàhp róht bpai tahm ngahn.
    ผมขับรถไปทำงาน I drive to work.

    Use 'mah' มา when a subject is heading toward the speaker.

    Ex. At work, his staff can say that,
    Jâo nah-ii kàhp róht mah tahm ngahn.
    เจ้านายขับรถมาทำงาน The boss drives to work.

4-5. To go upstairs is 'kêun bahn dai' ขึ้นบันได and to go downstairs is 'lohng bahn dai' ลงบันได. These words are usually used in combination with 'bpai' ไป or 'mah' มา.
    For instance, A is telling B to come to the second floor.

    If A is on the second floor and B is on the first floor.

A says: Kêun mah cháhn sǎwng. ขึ้นมาชั้นสอง

If A and B are on the first floor,
A says: Kêun bpai cháhn sǎwng. ขึ้นไปชั้นสอง

If A and B are on upper floor,
A says: Lohng bpai cháhn sǎwng. ลงไปชั้นสอง

If A is on the second floor and B is on the upper floor,
A says: Lohng mah cháhn sǎwng. ลงมาชั้นสอง

6 When referring to ordinal numbers, add the word 'tîi' ที่ in front of the number. Thus 'the first' is 'tîi nèung' ที่หนึ่ง, the second is 'tîi sǎwng' ที่สอง and so on.
If there is a noun, put the noun in front of 'tîi ที่ + number'.
When referring to floors/stories of a building, Thais sometimes like to omit 'tîi' ที่.
Ex. Cháhn (tîi) sǎwng ชั้น(ที่)สอง (The second floor)

Compare: 'two floors' in Thai is 'sǎwng cháhn' สองชั้น

For other situations, it is best to retain the word 'tîi' in front of the number referred to.
Ex. Sìi yâek tîi sǎhm สี่แยกที่สาม (The third intersection)
Ex. Hâwng tîi sìi ห้องที่สี่ (The fourth room).

DRILLS

1. Practice telling directions by completing the following phrase with the words provided below.
Tĕung ถึง __A__ , léaw แล้ว __B__.'
When you reach __A__, then __B__ .

A. fai daeng	ไฟแดง	(red) traffic light
B. líaw sáh-ii	เลี้ยวซ้าย	turn left
A. tahng yâek	ทางแยก	intersection
B. líaw kwăh	เลี้ยวขวา	turn right
A. sàh pahn law-ii	สะพานลอย	pedestrian bridge ("floating bridge")
B. glàhp róht	กลับรถ	U-turn
A. sàh pahn	สะพาน	bridge
B. jàwt	จอด	stop the car

2. To find out if there is a particular place nearby, ask; 'Tăew níi mii....maí?' แถวนี้มี....มั้ย? *Is there a....around here?* Practice this structure by completing the above sentence with the following words.

ráhn dtàht pŏhm	ร้านตัดผม	salon, barbershop
ráhn dtàht sêua	ร้านตัดเสื้อ	tailor
ráhn kăh-ii yah	ร้านขายยา	pharmacy
sàh tăh nii dtahm rùat	สถานีตำรวจ	police station
sàh tăh nii róht fai fáh	สถานีรถไฟฟ้า	sky-train station
rohng pah yah bahn	โรงพยาบาล	hospital

3. To ask where a place is located, say:
'.... yòo tîi năi? ....อยู่ที่ไหน? *Where is ....?*

To ask directions to that place, say:
'.... bpai tahng năi? ....ไปทางไหน? *Which way to....?*

To ask how to get to that place, (i.e., the means of transportation such as boat, taxi, or walk), say:
'.... bpai yahng ngai? ....ไปยังไง? *How to go to....?*

Practice these structures by completing the above sentences with the words provided below.

Dt<u>èu</u>k <u>a</u>h sòhk	ตึกอโศก	Asoke building
S<u>à</u>h năhm bin	สนามบิน	airport
Bp<u>á</u>hm n<u>á</u>hm m<u>a</u>hn	ปั๊มน้ำมัน	gasoline station
Rohng raem	โรงแรม	hotel
S<u>à</u>h tăhn tôot wîat nahm	สถานทูตเวียดนาม	Vietnamese Embassy

4. Practice telling location by completing the following sentence with the words provided below.

'Rohng raem hil dt<u>â</u>hn yòo....dt<u>èu</u>k Asoke.'
โรงแรมฮิลตันอยู่....ตึกอโศก. *Hilton Hotel is....the Asoke building.*

glai jàhk	ไกลจาก	far from
glâi g<u>à</u>hp	ใกล้กับ	close to
dtìt g<u>à</u>hp	ติดกับ	next to
kâhng (kâhng)	ข้างๆ	at the side
kâhng nâh	ข้างหน้า	in front (of)
kâhng l<u>ă</u>hng	ข้างหลัง	at the back (of)
kâhng b<u>o</u>hn	ข้างบน	on top of, upstairs
kâhng lâhng	ข้างล่าง	at the bottom (of), downstairs
kâhng sáh-ii	ข้างซ้าย	on the left
kâhng kwăh	ข้างขวา	on the right
dtr<u>o</u>hng glahng	ตรงกลาง	in the middle
gàwn	ก่อน	before
l<u>ă</u>hng	หลัง	after
dtr<u>o</u>hng kâhm	ตรงข้าม	opposite
f<u>à</u>hng dtr<u>o</u>hng kâhm	ฝั่งตรงข้าม	the opposite side

EXERCISES

1. What do you say in Thai when...
   A. You want to find out if a place is far away.
   B. You do not want the taxi driver to take the expressway.
   C. You want to find out where you can get a taxi.
   D. You want to find out if the sky-train passes Phyathai hospital.
   E. You are in a taxi and the taxi driver just drove past your destination.
   F. You want the taxi driver to go to the left lane.
   G. You want the taxi driver to go to the right lane.
   H. You want the taxi driver to stay in the middle lane.
   I. You want to ask the driver to drive slower.
   J. You want to ask the driver to stop at the traffic light.

2. How do you say the following sentences in Thai?
   A. To Bumrungrad Hospital, please.
   B. Please take the express way.
   C. Please turn left at the intersection.
   D. Please turn right at the traffic light.
   E. Please stop at the pedestrian bridge.
   F. Go straight and then turn right at the intersection.
   G. The restaurant is on the right.
   H. The building is ahead.

3. Translate the following sentences into English.
   A. Bpai jàh dtòo jàhk lohng tîi sàh tăh nii arai? ไปจะต้องจากลงที่สถานีอะไร?

B. Bpai s<u>eh</u>n tâhn chít l<u>oh</u>m l<u>oh</u>ng tîi bpâh-ii r<u>óh</u>t meh nǎi? ไปเซ็นทรัลชิดลมลงที่ป้ายรถเมล์ไหน?
C. Pàhn t<u>àh</u> n<u>ŏh</u>n pr<u>áh</u> rahm sìi mái? ผ่านถนนพระรามสี่มั้ย?
D. Bpai s<u>òo</u>t saw-ii. ไปสุดซอย
E. De(r)n kâhm t<u>àh</u> n<u>ŏh</u>n bpai f<u>àh</u>ng dtr<u>oh</u>ng kâhm. เดินข้ามถนนไปฝั่งตรงข้าม
F. Líaw kwǎh tîi sìi yâek tîi sǎhm. เลี้ยวขวาที่สี่แยกที่สาม
G. K<u>êu</u>n b<u>ah</u>n dai bpai láew líaw sáh-ii. ขึ้นบันไดไปแล้วเลี้ยวซ้าย
H. Kâhm s<u>àh</u> pahn, láew jàwt. ข้ามสะพานแล้วจอด

The colloquial Thai way of telling the time of day uses a variety of systems. The word 'dtii', meaning 'to strike', is used for telling the time after mid-night and before six a.m. 'Mohng' is used for the daylight hours and 'tôom' is used to denote the evening hours until midnight. It is believed that these words originate from the sounds of bells, gongs and drums. The formal system of telling time follows the standard 24-hour clock. In this system, the Thai language uses the word 'na-li-gaa' meaning 'clock' to tell the time.

Thai day names relate to the gods of the planets in ancient Indian astrology, and each day has a color. In the past, some Thai people believed that the color of the day impacts many things and they would factor in the day's color when getting dressed in the morning.

Sunday is red for the sun god, Monday is yellow for the moon god, Tuesday is pink for the Mars god, Wednesday is green for the Mercury god, Thursday is orange for the Jupiter god, Friday is blue for the Venus god, and Saturday is violet for the Saturn god.

There are many taboos and beliefs about certain activities on each particular day. One of the well-known taboos among older generations is that you should not have a hair-cut on Wednesday, which explains why some hairdressers close on Wednesdays. The years in Thai are counted according to the Buddhist era which is 543 years ahead of the Christian era.

9. Telling Time

VOCABULARY

w<u>a</u>hn	วัน	day
w<u>a</u>hn j<u>a</u>hn	วันจันทร์	Monday
w<u>a</u>hn <u>a</u>hng kahn	วันอังคาร	Tuesday
w<u>a</u>hn póot	วันพุธ	Wednesday
w<u>a</u>hn páh réu hàht	วันพฤหัส	Thursday
w<u>a</u>hn sòok	วันศุกร์	Friday
w<u>a</u>hn sǎo	วันเสาร์	Saturday
w<u>a</u>hn ah tít	วันอาทิตย์	Sunday
w<u>a</u>hn yòot	วันหยุด	holiday
w<u>a</u>hn tîi	วันที่	date
w<u>a</u>hn níi	วันนี้	today
mêua wahn níi	เมื่อวานนี้	yesterday
mêua gîi níi	เมื่อกี้นี้	just now
prôong níi	พรุ่งนี้	tomorrow
sǎhm w<u>a</u>hn gàwn	สามวันก่อน	three days ago
ìik sǎhm w<u>a</u>hn	อีกสามวัน	another three days
w<u>a</u>hn gè(r)t	วันเกิด	birthday
ah tít	อาทิตย์	week
ah tít níi	อาทิตย์นี้	this week
ah tít tîi láew	อาทิตย์ที่แล้ว	last week
sǎhm ah tít gàwn	สามอาทิตย์ก่อน	three weeks ago
ìik sǎhm ah tít	อีกสามอาทิตย์	another three weeks

deuan	เดือน	month[1]
móhk gàh rah kohm	มกราคม	January
goom pah pahn	กุมภาพันธ์	February
mii nah kohm	มีนาคม	March
meh săh yohn	เมษายน	April
préut sàh pah kohm	พฤษภาคม	May
mí tòo nah yohn	มิถุนายน	June
gàh ráh gàh dah kohm	กรกฎาคม	July
sĭng hăh kohm	สิงหาคม	August
gahn yah yohn	กันยายน	September
dtòo lah kohm	ตุลาคม	October
préut sàh jì gah yohn	พฤศจิกายน	November
tahn wah kohm	ธันวาคม	December
deuan níi	เดือนนี้	this month
deuan tîi láew	เดือนที่แล้ว	last month
săhm deuan gàwn	สามเดือนก่อน	3 months ago
ìik săhm deuan	อีกสามเดือน	another 3 months
bpii	ปี	year
bpii níi	ปีนี้	this year
bpii tîi láew	ปีที่แล้ว	last year
săhm bpii gàwn	สามปีก่อน	3 years ago
ìik săhm bpii	อีกสามปี	another 3 years
weh lah	เวลา	time
mohng	โมง	o'clock[2]
dtawn	ตอน	at (or 'in', a preposition used to indicate time)[3]
dtawn hòhk mohng	ตอนหกโมง	at six o'clock
chûa mohng	ชั่วโมง	hour

nah tii	นาที	minute
krêung	ครึ่ง	half
cháh-oo	เช้า	morning
dtawn cháh-oo	ตอนเช้า	in the morning
ah hăhn cháh-oo	อาหารเช้า	breakfast
bàh-ii	บ่าย	afternoon
yehn	เย็น	late afternoon
ah hăhn yehn	อาหารเย็น	dinner
glahng wahn	กลางวัน	day-time
ah hăhn glahng wahn	อาหารกลางวัน	lunch
glahng keun	กลางคืน	night-time
tîang (wahn)	เที่ยง(วัน)	noon
tîang keun	เที่ยงคืน	midnight
nahn	นาน	long (time)[4]

DIALOGUE

1. A: Wahn níi wahn arai káh?
   วันนี้วันอะไรคะ? What day is today?

   B: (Wahn níi) wahn jahn kráhp.
   (วันนี้) วันจันทร์ครับ (Today is) Monday.

2. A: Wahn níi wahn tîi tâo rai káh?
   วันนี้วันที่เท่าไรคะ? What date is today?

   B: (Wahn níi wahn tîi) sìp hâh kráhp.
   (วันนี้วันที่) สิบห้าครับ (Today is) the 15th.

3. A: Gìi mohng láew káh?
   กี่โมงแล้วคะ? What time is it?

   B: Sìi mohng krêung (láew) kráhp.
   สี่โมงครึ่ง (แล้ว) ครับ Half past four (already).

4. A: Bpòhk gàh dtì tahn ah hăhn yehn gìi mohng káh?
   ปกติทานอาหารเย็นกี่โมงคะ? What time do you normally have dinner?
   B: Bpràh mahn hòhk mohng sìp nah tii kráhp.
   ประมาณหกโมงสิบนาทีครับ Around six o'clock ten minutes.

GRAMMAR NOTES

1. 'Deuan' เดือน ending with 'kohm' คม have 31 days and those ending with 'yohn' ยน have 30 days.

2. From 6 a.m. until before noon, say:
   number + 'mohng' โมง + 'cháh-oo' เช้า
   Ex. Jèht mohng cháh-oo เจ็ดโมงเช้า 7 a.m.

   At noon, say:

   'tîang wahn' เที่ยงวัน or 'sìp săwng mohng' สิบสองโมง 12 o'clock

   From 1 p.m. until before 5 p.m., say:
   'bàh-ii' บ่าย + number + 'mohng' โมง
   Ex. Bàh-ii săwng mohng บ่ายสองโมง 2 p.m.

   From 5 p.m. until before 7 p.m., say:
   number + 'mohng' โมง + 'yehn' เย็น
   Ex. Hâh mohng yehn ห้าโมงเย็น 5 p.m.

   From 7 p.m. until before mid-night, say:

7 p.m.	= nèung tôom	หนึ่งทุ่ม
8 p.m.	= săwng tôom	สองทุ่ม
9 p.m.	= săhm tôom	สามทุ่ม

10 p.m. = sìi tôom   สี่ทุ่ม
11 p.m. = hâh tôom   ห้าทุ่ม

At mid-night, say: 'tîang keun' เที่ยงคืน

From 1 a.m. until before 6 a.m., say:
'dtii' ตี + number
Ex. dtii 3 ตีสาม 3 a.m.

3. Use the word 'dtawn' ตอน as a preposition (equivalent to 'at' or 'in' in English) used before a noun to indicate time.

dtawn cháh-oo	ตอนเช้า	in the morning
dtawn bàh-ii	ตอนบ่าย	in the afternoon
dtawn glahng keun	ตอนกลางคืน	at night
dtawn sìi mohng	ตอนสี่โมง	at 4 o'clock

4. Use '(chái weh lah) nahn tâo rai?' นานเท่าไร? or '(chái weh lah) nahn kâe năi?' นานแค่ไหน? at the end of a sentence when asking about the length of time it takes to do something.

Ex. Bpai poo gèht chái weh lah nahn tâo rai?
ไปภูเก็ตใช้เวลานานเท่าไร? How long does it take to go to Phuket?

If you want to ask 'how long have you...?', say: '...nahn kâe năi láew?' ...นานแค่ไหนแล้ว?

Ex. Koon yòo tîi nîi nahn kâe năi láew?
คุณอยู่ที่นี่นานแค่ไหนแล้ว? How long have you been here?

Ex. Káo raw koon nahn kâe năi láew?
เค้ารอคุณนานแค่ไหนแล้ว? How long has he/she been waiting for you?

'Kâe năi?' แค่ไหน after an adjective or adverb means 'how + adjective/adverb?'

pèht kâe năi	เผ็ดแค่ไหน	how spicy?
dii kâe năi	ดีแค่ไหน	how good?
yâhk kâe năi	ยากแค่ไหน	how difficult?

DRILLS

1. Practice asking times by completing the following sentence using the list of verbs provided: 'Wahn níi koon (verb) dtawn gìi mohng?' วันนี้คุณ....ตอนกี่โมง? *What time do you....today?*

rian pah săh tai	เรียนภาษาไทย	study Thai
àhn năhng sĕu	อ่านหนังสือ	read a book
de(r)n lêhn	เดินเล่น	have a walk
bpai tîaw	ไปเที่ยว	go out for fun
lêhn gii lah	เล่นกีฬา	play sports
bpìt tii wii	ปิดทีวี	turn off the TV
pôot toh rah sàhp	พูดโทรศัพท์	talk on the phone

2. Answer drill 1 by completing the following phrase with the time words provided: 'Dtawn....'. ตอน...... *At.....*

dtii nèung krêung	ตีหนึ่งครึ่ง	01:30
hòhk mohng cháh-oo yîi sìp (nah tii)	หกโมงเช้ายี่สิบ (นาที)	06:20
bpàet mohng cháh-oo	แปดโมงเช้า	08:00
tîang sìi sìp (nah tii)	เที่ยงสี่สิบ(นาที)	12:40
bàh-ii săwng mohng krêung	บ่ายสองโมงครึ่ง	14:30
hâh mohng yen sìp hâh	ห้าโมงเย็นสิบห้า	17:15

hâh (nah tii)   (นาที)
sìi tôom krêung   สี่ทุ่มครึ่ง   22:30

3. Practice '....kâe nǎi?' ....แค่ไหน? *How*....?, by completing the phrase with the following words.

glai	ไกล	far
glâi	ใกล้	near
sǒong	สูง	high, tall
yah-oo	ยาว	long
sâhn	สั้น	short
ûan	อ้วน	fat
pǎwm	ผอม	thin

EXERCISES

1. Find an English equivalent.
   A. Sìi mohng yehn wahn níi. สี่โมงเย็นวันนี้
   B. Dtii sǎhm prôong níi. ตีสามพรุ่งนี้
   C. mêua wahn níi bàh-ii nèung mohng yîi sìp
      เมื่อวานนี้บ่ายหนึ่งโมงยี่สิบ
   D. Wahn ah tít dtawn sǎwng tôom วันอาทิตย์ตอนสองทุ่ม
   E. Wahn sòok dtawn hòhk mohng yehn. วันศุกร์ตอนหกโมงเย็น
   F. Nèung tôom wahn ahng kahn หนึ่งทุ่มวันอังคาร
   G. Tîang keun sìi sìp nah tii เที่ยงคืนสี่สิบนาที
   H. Tîang krêung เที่ยงครึ่ง

2. Find a Thai equivalent.
   A. What time is it?
   B. What month is it?

C. What day is it?
   D. What year is it?
   E. 12:45
   F. 16:20
   G. 22:30
   H. 04:10

3. What do you say when...
   A. You want to know how far it is to the Hilton Hotel.
   B. You want to know how far it is to Pattaya.
   C. You want to know how spicy the food is.
   D. You want to know how big her house is.
   E. You want to know how small his office is.
   F. You want to know how hot the weather is.
   G. You want to know how cold the weather is.
   H. You want to know how long her hair is.

Do not expect Thai people to show up on time, due to traffic congestion and other excuses. You may find that Thai people adhere to times and schedules less strictly and more flexibly than Westerners. When making an appointment with an electrician, a plumber, a mechanic, etc, it is possible that they will be late for hours or don't show up at all.

Thai people also often pay their friends or family a visit without making an appointment in advance. And it is not considered rude, especially in the provinces, to drop-by at meal times.

Generally speaking, medical practitioners, barbers, tailors and many service providers do not require an advance appointment.

10. Appointments

VOCABULARY

náht	นัด	an appointment, to make an appointment
mii náht	มีนัด	to have an appointment
pìt náht	ผิดนัด	to miss an appointment
náht + someone + wái	นัด....ไว้	to have made an appointment with someone
mah săh-ii	มาสาย	to come late
mah reh-oo	มาเร็ว	to come early
mah dtrohng weh lah	มาตรงเวลา	to come straight on time
mah tahn weh lah	มาทันเวลา	to come in time
chûay....nàw-ii	ช่วย....หน่อย	please....[1]
(verb) + hâi + someone	ให้	(to do something) for someone
bàwk	บอก	to tell
bàwk + someone + wâh	บอก....ว่า	to tell someone that
je(r)	เจอ	to meet
gahn	กัน	each other, mutually (adv.)
je(r) gahn	เจอกัน	to meet each other
wahn níi	วันนี้	today
kít	คิด	to think
kít wâh	คิดว่า	to think that[2]
róht dtìt	รถติด	traffic jam

nahn	นาน	long (time)
bpràh mahn	ประมาณ	approximately
yóhk lê(r)k	ยกเลิก	to cancel
dtâwng	ต้อง	must
raw	รอ	to wait
dtèun nawn	ตื่นนอน	to wake up
ngûang nawn	ง่วงนอน	sleepy
àhn	อ่าน	to read
măw	หมอ	doctor
măw fahn	หมอฟัน	dentist
năhng sĕu pim	หนังสือพิมพ์	newspaper

DIALOGUE

Sam: Koon nit, chûay náht koon jŏom haî pŏhm nàw-ii kráhp. Bàwk káo wâh, je(r) gahn wahn níi, dtawn săhm tôom tîi Starbucks.
คุณนิด ช่วยนัดคุณจุ๋มให้ผมหน่อยครับ บอกเค้าว่าเจอกันวันนี้ตอนสามทุ่มที่สตาร์บัคส์
Khun Nit, please make an appointment with khun Joom for me. Tell her that I will meet her today at 9 p.m. at Starbucks.

Nit: Dâi kàh.
ได้ค่ะ OK.

Nit is calling Pat, Jŏom's secretary.

Nit: Koon paét káh, koon saem kăw náht[3] koon jŏom, wahn níi dtawn săhm tôom tîi Starbucks kàh.
คุณแพ็ทคะ คุณแซมขอนัดคุณจุ๋มวันนี้ตอนสามทุ่มที่สตาร์บัคส์ค่ะ
Khun Pat, khun Sam would like to make an appointment with khun Joom today at 9 p.m. at Starbucks.

Pat: Dâi kàh. Di cháhn jàh bàwk káo hâi (koon).
ได้ค่ะ ดิฉันจะบอกเค้าให้(คุณ) Ok. I will tell him (for you).

At Starbucks.

Sam: Kăw tôht kráhp koon jŏom, pŏhm mah săh-ii (bpai) yîi sìp nah tii.[4]
ขอโทษครับคุณจุ๋ม ผมมาสาย(ไป) ยี่สิบนาที Khun Joom, I'm sorry. I am 20 minutes late.

Jŏom: Cháhn kít wâh koon jàh mâi mah.
ฉันคิดว่าคุณจะไม่มา I thought you wouldn't come.

Sam: Wahn níi róht dtìt mâhk kráhp. Koon mah nahn réu yahng[5] kráhp?
วันนี้รถติดมากครับ คุณมานานรึยังครับ? Traffic is very bad today. Have you been here long?

Jŏom: Nahn láew[6] kàh, bpràh mahn sìp hâh nah tii.
นานแล้วค่ะ ประมาณสิบห้านาที Yes, around 15 minutes.

GRAMMAR NOTES

[1] 'Chûay + verb + ...(hâi) nàw-ii' ช่วย....(ให้) หน่อย is used when you want to request someone to do something. 'hâi nàw-ii' ให้หน่อย, literally means 'for (me)', showing a sense of gentleness.
You may add the word 'dâi mái?' ได้มั้ย? Could/can you? at the end of a sentence making it more polite.

Ex. Chûay bpè(r)t bpràh dtoo hâi nàw-ii kàh.
ช่วยเปิดประตูให้หน่อยค่ะ Please open the door for me.

Ex. Chûay tĕu tŏong hâi nàw-ii kàh.
ช่วยถือถุงให้หน่อยค่ะ Please hold the bag for me.

Ex. Chûay séu gah fae hâi nàw-ii kàh.
ช่วยซื้อกาแฟให้หน่อยค่ะ Please buy me a coffee.

Ex. Chûay pôot cháh cháh nàw-ii (dâi mái?) kráhp.
ช่วยพูดช้าๆ หน่อย (ได้มั้ย?)ครับ (Could you?) speak slowly please.

Ex. Chûay náht koon jim hâi nàw-ii (dâi mái?) kráhp.
ช่วยนัดคุณจิมให้หน่อย(ได้มั้ย?)ครับ (Could you?) make an appointment with khun Jim for (me).

2 'Wâh' ว่า as a verb means 'to say' or 'to criticize' but the common use of 'wâh' is as a conjunction introducing a substantial clause after verbs of mental action such as 'kít' คิด (*think*), 'chêua' เชื่อ (*believe*), 'kâo jai' เข้าใจ (*understand*), 'săhn yah' สัญญา (*promise*), róo รู้ (*know*), pôot พูด (*say*), róo sèuk รู้สึก (*feel*). In this usage, it is similar to the English conjunction 'that'.

Ex. Pŏhm kít wâh káo mâi sah bah-ii.
ผมคิดว่าเค้าไม่สบาย I think/thought he is sick.

Ex. Káo pôot wâh 'kăw tôht'.
เค้าพูดว่า(ขอโทษ) He says/said 'sorry'.

Ex. Koon jim bàwk pŏhm wâh wahn níi jàh mâi mah.
คุณจิมบอกผมว่าวันนี้จะไม่มา Khun Jim told me that he will not come today.

Ex. Bàwk káo wâh pŏhm mâi wâhng.
บอกเค้าว่าผมไม่ว่าง Tell him that I am not free.

Ex. Koon kâo jai wâh yahng ngai?
คุณเข้าใจว่ายังไง? What do you understand by that?

Ex. Chăhn róo wâh koon dii jai.
ฉันรู้ว่าคุณดีใจ I know that you are glad.

Ex. Káo tăhm wâh koon hĭw mái?
เค้าถามว่าคุณหิวมั้ย? He asks/asked if you are hungry.

3 Use 'Di cháhn/pŏhm kăw náht + koon... + nàw-ii kàh/ kráhp' ดิฉัน/ผมขอนัดคุณ...หน่อยค่ะ/ครับ when you, yourself, want

to make an appointment with someone. This is equivalent to 'May I make an appointment with khun...?'

Ex. Pŏhm kăw náht koon măw prôong níi hâh mohng yehn. ผมขอนัดคุณหมอพรุ่งนี้ห้าโมงเย็น I would like to make an appointment with the doctor at 5 p.m. tomorrow.

4 To inform someone how long you are going to be late, place the time word after 'jàh mah săh-ii' จะมาสาย.

Ex. Pŏhm jàh mah săh-ii hâh nah tii
ผมจะมาสายห้านาที I will be five minutes late.

5-6 'Réu yahng?' รึยัง? (short form is 'yahng?' ยัง? and full form is 'láew réu yahng?' แล้วรึยัง?), literally means 'already or not yet?', is a question word used similarly to 'have you..?' or 'are you...yet?'. It is often used to find out if the action is completed or not.

To answer Yes: (repeat) the verb + láew แล้ว = yes, already.
To answer No: yahng ยัง + mâi ไม่ + verb
      Or : yahng ยัง (in a short form) = not yet.

Ex. Tahn kâh-oo láew réu yahng káh?
ทานข้าวแล้วรึยังคะ? Have you eaten yet?
Yes: Tahn láew ทานแล้ว
No: Yahng mâi tahn ยังไม่ทาน

Ex. Sèht réu yahng káh?
เสร็จรึยังคะ? Are you finished?
Yes: Sèht láew เสร็จแล้ว
No: Yahng mâi sèht ยังไม่เสร็จ

'Ke(r)-ii + verb....réu yahng?' เคย....รึยัง? or 'Ke(r)-ii + verb.... mái?' เคย....มั้ย?, literally mean 'Have you ever....?

To answer Yes: ke(r)-ii เคย + láew แล้ว.
To answer No: yahng ยัง + mâi ไม่ + ke(r)-ii เคย
Ex. Ke(r)-ii bpai sǐng kah bpoh mái? เคยไปสิงคโปร์มั้ย?
   Yes: Ke(r)-ii láew. เคยแล้ว
   No: Yahng mâi ke(r)-ii. ยังไม่เคย

'Ke(r)-ii' เคย means 'ever, used to, have done before' while 'mâi ke(r)-ii' ไม่เคย means 'never'.
Ex. Pǒhm ke(r)-ii lêhn bpian noh dtàe mâi ke(r)-ii lêhn gii dtâh. ผมเคยเล่นเปียนโนแต่ไม่เคยเล่นกีต้าร์
   I used to play the piano but I have never played the guitar.

DRILLS

1. Practice 'Chûay___nàw-ii?' ช่วย___หน่อย? *Could you please___?* by completing the phrase using the following words.

bpè(r)t bpràh dtoo	เปิดประตู	open the door
bpè(r)t ae	เปิดแอร์	turn on the airconditioner
pôot bao bao	พูดเบาๆ	speak softly
pôot cháh cháh	พูดช้าๆ	speak slowly
hǎh táek sîi	หาแท็กซี่	find a taxi
bpai dtàh làht	ไปตลาด	go to the market
tahm ah hǎhn	ทำอาหาร	cook
tahm kwahm sàh àht	ทำความสะอาด	clean

2. Practice '___réu yahng?' รึยัง? *Have you___?* or *Are you___yet?*
   '___láew' แล้ว *Yes, already.*
   'yahng mâi ___' ยังไม่ *Not yet.*
   by completing the phrases using the following words.

bpràh choom	ประชุม	have a meeting
àhp náhm	อาบน้ำ	bathe/shower
doo TV	ดูทีวี	watch TV
sàhng ah hăhn	สั่งอาหาร	order food
jàh-ii nge(r)n	จ่ายเงิน	pay (money)
sèht	เสร็จ	finished
mah tĕung	มาถึง	arrive
séu kăwng	ซื้อของ	buy things/shopping

3. Practice 'Ke(r)-ii___láew réu yahng? เคย___แล้วรึยัง? *Have you ever___?*
   'Ke(r)-ii láew' เคยแล้ว *Yes, I have.*
   'yahng mâi ke(r)-ii' ยังไม่เคย *No, not yet.*
by completing the phrase using the following words.

lêhn golf	เล่นกอล์ฟ	play golf
fahng dohn dtrii	ฟังดนตรี	listen to music
bpai doo năhng	ไปดูหนัง	go to the movies
láhng róht	ล้างรถ	wash a car
ah rohm dii	อารมณ์ดี	(to be in a) good mood
ah rohm sĭa	อารมณ์เสีย	(to be in a) bad mood

EXERCISES

1. Translate the following sentences into English.

   A. Chûay náht koon soo sahn haî pŏhm nàw-ii kráhp.
   ช่วยนัดคุณซูซานให้ผมหน่อยครับ

   B. Bàwk káo wâh je(r) gahn prôong níi dtawn sìi tôom.
   บอกเค้าว่าเจอกันพรุ่งนี้ตอนสี่ทุ่ม

C. Bàwk káo wâh soo sahn yóhk lê(r)k náht wahn níi.
บอกเค้าว่าซูซานยกเลิกนัดวันนี้

D. Pŏhm kít wâh koon jàh mah săh-ii.
ผมคิดว่าคุณจะมาสาย

E. Wahn níi róht dtìt mâhk mái kráhp?
วันนี้รถติดมากมั้ยครับ?

F. Káo mah nahn réu yahng kráhp?
เค้ามานานรึยังครับ?

G. Yahng maî nahn kráhp.
ยังไม่นานครับ

H. Bpràh mahn yîi sìp nah tii
ประมาณยี่สิบนาที

I. Ke(r)-ii mah tîi nîi réu yahng káh?
เคยมาที่นี่รึยังคะ?

J. Dì cháhn mâi ke(r)-ii je(r) káo.
ดิฉันไม่เคยเจอเค้า

2. How do you say the following sentences in Thai?
   A. Please make an appointment with khun Sam for me.
   B. Please make an appointment with a dentist at Bumrungrad Hospital for me.
   C. Sorry I am late.
   D. See you (meet each other) tomorrow.
   E. See you (meet each other) at home at 5 o'clock.
   F. I have made an appointment with Khun Sam.
   G. I have made an appointment with him.
   H. Have you made an appointment yet?
   I. Tell him that I will be 15 minutes late.

J. Tell him that I have to cancel the appointment.
K. Have you ever been to Phuket?
L. I have never played football.

3. How do you answer 'Yes' and 'No' to the following sentences?

   A. Náht koon saem réu yahng káh?
      นัดคุณแซมรึยังคะ?

   B. Mii náht réu yahng káh?
      มีนัดรึยังคะ?

   C. Raw nahn réu yahng káh?
      รอนานรึยังคะ?

   D. Bàwk káo réu yahng káh?
      บอกเค้ารึยังคะ?

   E. Bpai dtàh làht réu yahng káh?
      ไปตลาดรึยังคะ?

   F. Dtèun nawn réu yahng káh?
      ตื่นนอนรึยังคะ?

   G. Ngûang nawn réu yahng káh?
      ง่วงนอนรึยังคะ?

   H. Gin kâh-oo réu yahng káh?
      กินข้าวรึยังคะ?

   I. Hĭw réu yahng káh?
      หิวรึยังคะ?

   J. Ke(r)-ii àhn năhng sĕu pim Bangkok Post mái?
      เคยอ่านหนังสือพิมพ์บางกอกโพสท์มั้ย?

   K. Ke(r)-ii bpai tahm ngahn săh-ii mái?
      เคยไปทำงานสายมั้ย?

It is not customary for Thai people to invite people home. Instead, they will entertain their guests at a restaurant. One of the reasons is that a Thai home is more of an extended family compound. Thus, it is not uncommon to see three generations living together in one house.

Also, Thai people prefer a slow and steady progress to a relationship. This explains why it is more difficult to make friends with Thai people than with Westerners. Once the relationship is solid, they may feel more comfortable to invite you home.

When Thai people have guests at home, water will almost automatically be served. Also, anyone arriving around mealtime is always welcome to stay and share the food.
When invited to a Thai home, don't walk into the house with footwear on. This is due to the fact that Thai people often sit, sleep and sometimes even eat on the floor.

11. Invitation

VOCABULARY

che(r)n	เชิญ	to invite someone formally[1]
chuan	ชวน	to invite someone informally/to ask someone to do something together[2]
wâhng	ว่าง	free, unoccupied
yôong	ยุ่ง	busy
(dûay) gahn	(ด้วย)กัน	together[3]
bpai tîaw	ไปเที่ยว	go out for fun/go on holiday
bpai de(r)n lêhn	ไปเดินเล่น	to stroll
doo năhng	ดูหนัง	to watch a movie
fahng	ฟัง	to listen
plehng	เพลง	song
fahng plehng	ฟังเพลง	to listen to music
ráwng plehng	ร้องเพลง	to sing a song
dtêhn rahm	เต้นรำ	to dance
doo kăwng	ดูของ	to have a look at merchandise, to window shop
tahn ah hăhn cháh-oo	ทานอาหารเช้า	to have breakfast
tahn ah hăhn glahng wahn	ทานอาหารกลางวัน	to have lunch
tahn ah hăhn yehn	ทานอาหารเย็น	to have dinner

ngahn líang	งานเลี้ยง	party
ngahn wahn gè(r)t	งานวันเกิด	birthday party
ngahn dtàeng ngahn	งานแต่งงาน	wedding party
tăew náhn	แถวนั้น	around there
tăew níi	แถวนี้	around here
dtàe	แต่	but

DIALOGUE

A: **Bàh-ii níi, wâhng mái kráhp?**
บ่ายนี้ว่างมั้ยครับ? Are you free this afternoon?

B: **Mâi wâhng kàh. Bàh-ii níi mii bpràh choom kàh.**
ไม่ว่างค่ะ บ่ายนี้มีประชุมค่ะ No, I am not free. I have a meeting this afternoon.

A: **Prôong níi làh kráhp?**
พรุ่งนี้ล่ะครับ? What about tomorrow?

B: **Prôong níi wâhng kàh. Tahm mai káh?**
พรุ่งนี้ว่างค่ะ ทำไมคะ? Tomorrow I am free, why?

A: **Jàh chuan bpai dtàh làht jàh dtòo jàhk dûay gahn nàw-ii kráhp. Bpai maí[4] kráhp?**
จะชวนไปตลาดจตุจักรด้วยกันหน่อยครับ ไปมั้ยครับ? I want to ask you to go to Jatujak market together. Do you want to go?

B: **Yàhk bpai gìi mohng káh?**
อยากไปกี่โมงคะ? What time do you want to go?

A: **Bàh-ii săhm mohng kráhp.**
บ่ายสามโมงครับ Three o'clock in the afternoon.

B: **Dâi kàh, je(r) gahn tîi năi dii[5] káh?**
ได้ค่ะ เจอกันที่ไหนดีคะ? OK. Where shall we meet?

A: Tîi kâhng nâh dtèuk Asoke dii mái kráhp?
ที่ข้างหน้าตึกอโศกดีมั้ยครับ? Shall we meet in front of Asoke Building?

B: Dii kàh. Rao jàh bpai yahng ngai dii káh?
ดีค่ะ เราจะไปยังไงดีคะ? Good. How shall we go?

A: Bpai róht fai fáh dii gwàh. Tăew náhn, róht dtìt mâhk.
ไปรถไฟฟ้าดีกว่า แถวนั้นรถติดมาก We better go by sky-train. The traffic around there is very bad.

B: Dâi kàh.
ได้ค่ะ OK.

GRAMMAR NOTES

1 To formally invite someone to do something promptly, say:
Che(r)n เชิญ + verb kàh/kráhp ค่ะ/ครับ.

   Ex. Che(r)n nâhng kàh/ kráhp.
   เชิญนั่งค่ะ/ครับ Please sit down.

   Ex. Che(r)n kâo mah kàh/ kráhp.
   เชิญเข้ามาค่ะ/ครับ Please come in.

   Ex. Che(r)n bpai gàwn kàh/ kráhp.
   เชิญไปก่อนค่ะ/ครับ Please go first/ahead.

To formally invite someone to go somewhere, say: Subject + kăw/yàhk che(r)n ขอ/อยาก เชิญ + someone + bpai ไป +.... nàw-ii kàh/ kráhp หน่อยค่ะ/ครับ

   Ex. Di cháhn kăw che(r)n koon bphai ngahn dtàeng ngahn di cháhn nàw-ii kàh.
   ดิฉันขอเชิญคุณไปงานแต่งงานดิฉันหน่อยค่ะ I would like to invite you to go to my wedding party.

   Ex. Pŏhm yàhk che(r)n koon bpai ngahn wahn gè(r)t pŏhm nàw-ii kráhp.
   ผมอยากเชิญคุณไปงานวันเกิดผมหน่อยครับ I would like to invite you to go to my birthday party.

² 'Chuan' ชวน is less formal than 'che(r)n' เชิญ but the usage is more or less the same. You may add 'gàhp pŏhm/di cháhn' กับผม/ดิฉัน (with me) or '(dûay) gahn' (ด้วย)กัน (together) at the end of the sentence.

   Ex. Pŏhm yàhk chuan koon bphai ngahn kêun bâhn mài pŏhm nàw-ii kráhp.
   ผมอยากชวนคุณไปงานขึ้นบ้านใหม่ผมหน่อยครับ I would like to ask you to go to my house warming party.

   Ex. Di cháhn yàhk chuan koon bpai séu kăwng gàhp di cháhn nàw-ii kàh.
   ดิฉันอยากชวนคุณไปซื้อของกับดิฉันหน่อยค่ะ I would like to ask you to go shopping with me.

³ To informally invite or persuade someone to do something or to go somewhere together, say; 'bpai ไป + verb + (dûay) gahn mái?' (ด้วย)กันมั้ย? 'Gahn' กัน is used to indicate that two or more people or things are mutually involved in the same activity.

   Ex. Bpai tîaw Pattaya gahn mái káh/kráhp?
   ไปเที่ยวพัทยากันมั้ยคะ/ครับ? Would you like to go to Pattaya together?

   Ex. Bpai gin kâh-oo gahn mái káh/kráhp?
   ไปกินข้าวกันมั้ยคะ/ครับ? Would you like to go and eat together?

   Ex. Bpai doo năhng gahn mái káh/kráhp?
   ไปดูหนังกันมั้ยคะ/ครับ? Would you like to go to the movies together?

⁴ To informally invite or persuade someone to do something promptly, say; verb + mái káh/kráhp มั้ยคะ/ครับ?

   Ex. Gin mái káh/kráhp?

Ex. กินมั้ยคะ/ครับ? Would you like to eat?
Ex. Nâhng mái káh/kráhp?
นั่งมั้ยคะ/ครับ? Would you like to sit down?

Ex. Lawng mái káh/kráhp?
ลองมั้ยคะ/ครับ? Would you like to try?

5 Use 'question word' + dii ดี at the end of the sentence when asking for someone's opinion.
Ex. Tahm arai dii?
ทำอะไรดี? What shall (we/I) do?
Ex. Lêhn tîi năi dii?
เล่นที่ไหน? Where shall (we/I) play?
Ex. De(r)n tahng mêua rai dii?
เดินทางเมื่อไรดี? When shall (we/I) travel?
Ex. Lêuak kohn năi dii?
เลือกคนไหนดี? Which person shall (we/I) choose?
Ex. Bpai gìi mohng dii?
ไปกี่โมงดี? What time shall (we/I) go?

DRILLS.

1. Practice 'Bpai___gahn mái káh/kráhp?' ไป___กันมั้ยคะ/ครับ? *Would you like to go ___ together?* by completing the sentence using the following words.

dahm náhm	ดำน้ำ	scuba diving
lêhn gii lah	เล่นกีฬา	play sport
àwk gahm lahng gah-ii	ออกกำลังกาย	exercise
de(r)n bpàh	เดินป่า	trek
rian pah săh tai	เรียนภาษาไทย	study Thai

2. Practice 'Di cháhn/Pŏhm + yàhk chuan + koon + bpai +___ dûay gahn nàw-ii kàh/kráhp'. ดิฉัน/ผมอยากชวนคุณไป___ด้วยกันหน่อยค่ะ/ครับ *I would like to invite you to* ___. by completing the sentence using the following words.

tahn ah hăhn	ทานอาหาร	eat
bâhn koon jim	บ้านคุณจิม	Khun Jim's house
ngahn líang	งานเลี้ยง	party
doo kăwng	ดูของ	window shopping
tàh-ii rôop	ถ่ายรูป	take a photo

EXERCISES

1. How do you say the following sentences in Thai?
    A. Where shall we go?
    B. What shall we do?
    C. When shall we meet?
    D. Where shall we sing?
    E. Where shall we eat?
    F. What movie shall we watch?
    G. Who shall we invite?

2. Please follow the instructions.
    A. Please ask your friend if he wants to join you for lunch.
    B. Decline an invitation and say you are very busy.
    C. Ask your friend if he is free on Sunday.
    D. Please invite your boss to join your wedding party.
    E. Please invite your friend to sit down.
    F. Please ask your friend if he wants to play golf with you tomorrow.
    G. Please invite a guest inside after opening the door.

It is not customary for Thai people to introduce themselves when answering the phone, especially when it concerns a private call. When making a phone call, Thai people sometimes like to confirm that they are calling the right place by asking the receiver's telephone number or the name of the place they are calling.

When calling a large company, you may get an automatic Thai-speaking answering machine. If the language is your barrier, you may try to wait for an operator who usually answers the phone after the recording. If it takes too long, try pressing zero or nine, you may get the operator faster.

12. Telephone Conversation

VOCABULARY

toh rah sàhp	โทรศัพท์	telephone (noun)
toh (rah sàhp)	โทร(ศัพท์)	to call
meu tĕu	มือถือ	mobile phone
be(r) toh rah sàhp	เบอร์โทรศัพท์	telephone number
be(r) meu tĕu	เบอร์มือถือ	mobile phone number
pìt	ผิด	wrong
toh pìt	โทรผิด	to call the wrong number
toh glàhp	โทรกลับ	to return a call, to call back
toh bpai hăh	โทรไปหา	to call someone (outgoing call)[1]
toh mah hăh	โทรมาหา	to call someone (incoming call)[2]
dtàw	ต่อ	extension
ráhp toh rah sàhp	รับโทรศัพท์	to pick up the phone
wahng hŏo	วางหู	to hang up the phone
tĕu săh-ii	ถือสาย	to hold the line
raw sáhk krôo	รอสักครู่	wait a moment
bàwk	บอก	to tell
bàwk káo wâh	บอกเค้าว่า	to tell him/her that
bàwk hâi + someone to do something	บอกให้	To tell someone to do something[3]
ìik tii / ìik kráhng	อีกที / อีกครั้ง	one more time
bàht toh rah sàhp	บัตรโทรศัพท์	telephone card

dĭaw	เดี๋ยว	hold on, just a minute[4]
gàhp	กับ	with, and
kăw pôot gàhp	ขอพูดกับ	May I speak with...
k<u>oo</u>n....yòo mái?	คุณ....อยู่มั้ย?	Is khun....there?
krai pôot?	ใครพูด?	Who is speaking?
wâhng	ว่าง	free, unoccupied
săh-ii	สาย	line (noun)
săh-ii mâi wâhng	สายไม่ว่าง	The line is busy.
ga<u>hm</u> la<u>hn</u>g + v.ing	กำลัง	to be v.ing (continuous tense)[5]

DIALOGUE

A: S<u>ah</u> w<u>àht</u> dii kàh. Tîi n<u>âh</u>n tîi năi k<u>áh</u>?
สวัสดีค่ะ ที่นั่นที่ไหนคะ? Hello. Where is that?

B: Nîi bâhn k<u>oo</u>n jim kr<u>áh</u>p.
นี่บ้านคุณจิมครับ This is Jim's house.

A: K<u>oo</u>n soo sahn yòo mái k<u>áh</u>?
คุณซูซานอยู่มั้ยคะ? Is khun Susan there?

B: Tĕu săh-ii raw s<u>áh</u>k krôo kr<u>áh</u>p....k<u>oo</u>n soo sahn mâi yòo kr<u>áh</u>p.
ถือสายรอสักครู่ครับ คุณซูซานไม่อยู่ครับ Wait a moment please. Khun Susan is not in.

A: Mii be(r) meu tĕu k<u>oo</u>n soo sahn mái k<u>áh</u>?
มีเบอร์มือถือคุณซูซานมั้ยคะ? Do you have khun Susan's mobile phone number?

B: Mâi mii kr<u>áh</u>p.
ไม่มีครับ No, I don't.

A: K<u>oo</u>n soo sahn j<u>àh</u> gl<u>àh</u>p mêua rài k<u>á</u>h?
คุณซูซานจะกลับเมื่อไรคะ? When will khun Susan be back?

B: Kít w<u>âh</u> dtawn sǎwng mohng kr<u>á</u>hp.
คิดว่าตอนสองโมงครับ I think at 2 o'clock.

A: Di ch<u>á</u>hn j<u>àh</u> toh bpai ìik tii dtawn sǎwng mohng k<u>àh</u>.
ดิฉันจะโทรไปอีกทีตอนสองโมงค่ะ I will call again at 2 o'clock.

B: Kǎw tôht kr<u>á</u>hp, krai (<u>gahm lahng</u>) pôot kr<u>á</u>hp?
ขอโทษ ใคร (กำลัง) พูดครับ? Excuse me, who is speaking?

A: Siri pôot k<u>àh</u>, di ch<u>á</u>hn toh j<u>àh</u>k tîi t<u>ah</u>m ngahn k<u>àh</u>.
สิริพูดค่ะ ดิฉันโทรจากที่ทำงานค่ะ Siri's speaking. I am calling from the office.

B: Be(r) toh r<u>ah</u> s<u>àh</u>p k<u>oo</u>n arai kr<u>á</u>hp?
เบอร์โทรศัพท์คุณอะไรครับ? What is your phone number?

A: Sǒon sǎwng sǎwng hâh j<u>èh</u>t sìi n<u>èu</u>ng sǎwng hâh, dtàw sìi sǎwng hâh k<u>àh</u>.
ศูนย์ สอง สอง ห้า เจ็ด สี่ หนึ่ง สอง ห้า ต่อ สี่ สอง ห้า ค่ะ 02-2574125 extension 425.

B: Pǒhm j<u>àh</u> b<u>àw</u>k k<u>oo</u>n soo sahn wâh k<u>oo</u>n toh mah.
ผมจะบอกคุณซูซานว่าคุณโทรมา
I will tell khun Susan that you called.

A: Kàwp k<u>oo</u>n k<u>àh</u>. S<u>ah</u> w<u>àh</u>t dii k<u>àh</u>.
ขอบคุณค่ะ สวัสดีค่ะ Thank you. Bye.

B: S<u>ah</u> w<u>àh</u>t dii kr<u>á</u>hp.
สวัสดีครับ Bye.

GRAMMAR NOTES

1-2 Use 'toh bpai hǎh' โทรไปหา for outgoing calls and and 'toh mah hǎh' โทรมาหา for incoming calls.

   Ex. P<u>ǒh</u>m toh bpai hǎh soo sahn.
   ผมโทรไปหาซูซาน I called Susan.

Ex. Soo sahn toh mah hăh pŏhm
ซูซานโทรมาหาผม Susan called me.

3 To leave a message for someone to call you back, say:
Bàwk hâi káo toh hăh di cháhn/pŏhm nàw-ii kàh/kráhp.'
บอกให้เค้าโทรหาดิฉัน/ผมหน่อยค่ะ/ครับ

Apply this structure:
'bàwk hâi บอกให้ + someone + to do something', when you want the person you are speaking to, to tell the third party to do something.

For instance, if you want your wife to tell your maid to cook Thai food tonight, say:

Bàwk hâi mâe bâhn tahm ah hăhn tai keun níi.
บอกให้แม่บ้านทำอาหารไทยคืนนี้

4 'dĭaw' เดี๋ยว when used alone, it means 'hold on/wait' but when used in front of a verb or a subject (if any), it means 'in just a moment, you will...'
Ex. Dĭaw pŏhm bpai   เดี๋ยวผมไป In just a moment I will go.
    Dĭaw mah   เดี๋ยวมา   In just a moment I will come.
    Dĭaw tahm   เดี๋ยวทำ   In just a moment I will do.

5 To indicate that the action is in progress, use 'gahm lahng' กำลัง in front of a verb and/or 'yòo' อยู่ behind a verb or at the end of the sentence. Its function is like the 'to be' + v.ing in English. Both 'gahm lahng' กำลัง and/or 'yòo' อยู่ are tense indicators.
There are three ways of saying: 'I am playing' in Thai.
1. gahm lahng lêhn yòo. กำลังเล่นอยู่

2. gahm lahng lêhn. กำลังเล่น

3. lêhn yòo. เล่นอยู่

However, in a circumstance that is clear to both parties, Thais sometimes skip these words completely.
For instance, when you see your friend trying to find something, you might say: 'hăh arai?' หาอะไร instead of 'hăh arai yòo?' หาอะไรอยู่? or 'gahm lahng hăh arai yòo?' กำลังหาอะไรอยู่? On the phone, to ask who is on the line, you may just say 'krai pôot káh/kráhp?' ใครพูดคะ/ครับ?

DRILLS

1. When asking for a telephone number, the short way to say is 'Be(r) toh rah sàhp arai?' เบอร์โทรศัพท์อะไร? Practice asking numbers by completing the phrase using the words below.
'Be(r)___arai?' เบอร์___อะไร?

fàek	แฟกซ์	fax
meu tĕu	มือถือ	mobile phone
toh rah sàhp tîi bâhn	โทรศัพท์ที่บ้าน	home phone
toh rah sàhp tîi tahm ngahn	โทรศัพท์ที่ทำงาน	office phone

2. To ask if one has telephone numbers of a certain place or person, say: 'Mii be(r)___mái?' มีเบอร์___มั้ย? Practice asking numbers by completing the phrase using the words below.

rohng pah yah bahn	โรงพยาบาล	hospital
rohng rian	โรงเรียน	school
rohng năhng	โรงหนัง	movie theatre
ráhn ah hăhn	ร้านอาหาร	restaurant

3. To leave a message for someone, say: 'Chûay bàwk káo wâh___' ช่วยบอกเค้าว่า___ *Please tell him/her that___* Practice this request by completing the sentence using the words below.

jim toh bpai (hăh)	จิมโทรไป(หา)	Jim called.
jim jàh toh bpai (hăh) ìik.	จิมจะโทรไป-(หา)อีก	Jim will call again.
jim jàh toh bpai (hăh) ìik nèung chûa mohng	จิมจะโทรไป(หา)-อีกหนึ่งชั่วโมง	Jim will call in one hour.
toh glàhp (hăh) jim	โทรกลับ(หา)จิม	Call Jim back.
toh glàhp (hăh) jim dtawn săhm mohng	โทรกลับ(หา)จิม-ตอนสามโมง	Call Jim back at 3 o'clock.

EXERCISES

1. What do you say when:
    A. You want the other line to wait.
    B. You want to speak to Jim.
    C. You want to leave a message for Susan to call you back.
    D. You want to know her mobile phone number.
    E. Someone calls the wrong number.
    F. You want the person on the line to call back in 2 hours.
    G. You want the person on the line to call back at 2 o'clock.
    H. You want the person on the phone to call back in the afternoon.

2. Follow the instructions.
    A. Call the restaurant and ask to talk to the manager (pôo jàht gahn ผู้จัดการ)

B. From A, the manager is not in, please ask the operator to tell the manager to call you back at 02-234-5678.
C. From A, the manager is not in, please ask the following:
- When will he be back?
- The manager's mobile phone number.
D. From A, the manager is not in, tell the operator that you will call him again in the afternoon.

Bathroom – It is wise to take your socks off before visiting the traditional Thai bathroom. Bathers ladle water with a plastic bowl from a built-in tank. Do not sit in the tank as you do in a western-style bath tub. Standing outside the tank, you bathe yourself by scooping water out of it and pouring it over the body. In the process, walls, floor and bathroom doors can be splashed. In the provinces, most bathrooms only have this type of water tank, and no shower.

Sacred room – Every Thai house has a room or at least a shelf for their sacred images to reside on. When sleeping, the residents point their feet away from these sacred sites and never point their heads towards the West. West is associated with death since Thai people generally bury their deceased by placing their heads to the West.

Spirit house – Most Thai people believe that a spirit house has to be erected when a building is constructed. This is to create a new home for the 'evicted' land spirits and to avoid bad luck for the property owner. Many, though not all, Thai houses locate their spirit houses outside the building but in the compound area. Sino-Thai people have a different style spirit house in red color. It is located inside the house facing the main door, its color is red.

13. Housekeeping

VOCABULARY

ngahn bâhn	งานบ้าน	housekeeping work
t<u>ah</u>m kwahm s<u>àh</u> àht	ทำความสะอาด	to clean
s<u>àh</u> àht	สะอาด	clean
s<u>òh</u>k g<u>àh</u> bpr<u>òh</u>k	สกปรก	dirty
pâh	ผ้า	cloth
s<u>á</u>hk pâh	ซักผ้า	to do laundry
s<u>á</u>hk hâeng	ซักแห้ง	to dry-clean
dtàhk pâh	ตากผ้า	to hang clothes to dry
rîit pâh	รีดผ้า	to iron
láhng jahn	ล้างจาน	to wash dishes
láhng r<u>ó</u>ht	ล้างรถ	to wash a car
jàht dt<u>ó</u>h	จัดโต๊ะ	to set a table
jàht kǎwng	จัดของ	to arrange/sort out things
gèhp kǎwng	เก็บของ	to put things in place
bplìan	เปลี่ยน	to change
nawn	นอน	to sleep, to lie down
tîi nawn	ที่นอน	a place to sleep, bed
pâh bpoo tîi nawn	ผ้าปูที่นอน	bed sheet
hâwng	ห้อง	room
hâwng nawn	ห้องนอน	bed room
n<u>â</u>hng	นั่ง	to sit
l<u>ê</u>hn	เล่น	to play

hâwng nâhng lêhn	ห้องนั่งเล่น	a living room
toh rah táht	โทรทัศน์	television
wít tah yóo	วิทยุ	radio
(hâwng) krua	(ห้อง)ครัว	kitchen
hâwng náhm	ห้องน้ำ	bathroom
dtôo	ตู้	cabinet
dtôo yehn	ตู้เย็น	refrigerator
dtóh	โต๊ะ	table, desk
gâo-îi	เก้าอี้	chair
bpràh dtoo	ประตู	door
nâh dtàhng	หน้าต่าง	window
pâh mâhn	ผ้าม่าน	curtain
prohm	พรม	carpet
jing jing	จริง จริง	really[1]
...lĕ(r)?	เหรอ?	question word?[2]
jàh + verb	จะ	will (future indicator)
dĭaw + verb	เดี๋ยว	in a moment
kàek	แขก	guest
gàwn	ก่อน	before
lăhng	หลัง	after
náh káh/náh kráhp	นะคะ/นะครับ?	OK?
sòhng	ส่ง	to send
ráhp	รับ	to pick up
dtriam	เตรียม	to prepare
rîak	เรียก	to call, to get (someone)
hĕhn	เห็น	to see
hăh	หา	to look for

je(r)	เจอ	to meet, to find
jai dii	ใจดี	kind
jai ráh-ii	ใจร้าย	cruel, mean (adj.)
bèua	เบื่อ	bored (adj.)

DIALOGUE

A: Daeng, yehn níi jàh mii kàek mah tahn ah hăhn yehn gàhp rao sìi kohn. Chûay tahm ah hăhn tai hâh yàhng nàw-ii náh kráhp?
แดง เย็นนี้จะมีแขกมาทานอาหารเย็นกับเราสี่คน ช่วยทำอาหารไทยห้าอย่างหน่อยนะครับ?
Daeng, there will be four guests coming to have dinner with us this evening. Could you cook 5 Thai dishes?

B: Dâi kàh. Kàek jàh mah gìi mohng káh?
ได้ค่ะ แขกจะมากี่โมงคะ? Yes. What time will the guests come?

A: Bpràh mahn hâh mohng yehn. Oh! Chûay tahm kwahm sàh àht hâwng nâhng lêhn, láew gâw jàht dtóh ah hăhn gàwn kàek mah náh kráhp. Pŏhm jáh bpai sòhng pâh, tîi ráhn sáhk hâeng, dĭaw mah.
ประมาณห้าโมงเย็น อ้อ! ช่วยทำความสะอาดห้องนั่งเล่น แล้วก็จัดโต๊ะอาหารก่อนแขกมานะครับ ผมจะไปส่งผ้าที่ร้านซักแห้ง เดี๋ยวมา
Around 5 p.m. Oh! Please clean the living room and set the dining table before they come. I am going to bring the clothes to the dry-cleaning shop and will be right back.

B: Mâi tahn ah hăhn glahng wahn gàwn lĕ(r) káh?
ไม่ทานอาหารกลางวันก่อนเหรอคะ? Aren't you going to have lunch first?

A: Yahng mâi hĭw kráhp[3]. Mêua cháh-oo níi tahn mâhk ge(r)n bpai[4]. Chûay bâwk hâi yahm rîak táek sîi hâi nàw-ii kráhp.

ยังไม่หิวครับ เมื่อเช้านี้ทานมากเกินไป ช่วยบอกให้ยามเรียกแท็กซี่ให้ หน่อยครับ
I am not hungry yet. I ate too much this morning. Could you tell the guard to call a taxi for me please?

B: Táek sîi mah láew kàh.
แท็กซี่มาแล้วค่ะ The taxi is here already.

A: Jing lĕ(r)? Bàwk yahm wâh pŏhm gahm lahng lohng bpai kráhp. Hĕhn gràh bpăo pŏhm mái kráhp? Mâi róo yòo tîi năi. Hăh mâi je(r)?[5]
จริงเหรอ? บอกยามว่าผมกำลังลงไปครับ เห็นกระเป๋าผมมั้ยครับ?
ไม่รู้อยู่ที่ไหน หาไม่เจอ Really? Tell the guard that I am on my way down. Have you seen my bag? I don't know where it is. I can't find it.

B: Kít wâh yòo nai dtôo kàh.
คิดว่าอยู่ในตู้ค่ะ I think it is in the cabinet.

A: Je(r) láew! Bpai gàwn náh, ìik săwng chûa mohng jàh glàhp mah.
เจอแล้ว! ไปก่อนนะ อีกสองชั่วโมงจะกลับมา I found it! I am going now and will return in two hours.

GRAMMAR NOTES

[1] 'Jing jing' จริงจริง (*really*), when placed after a verb or adjective acts as an adverb.

Ex. Káo châwp koon jing jing.
เค้าชอบคุณจริงจริง He really likes you.

Ex. Koon jai dii jing jing.
คุณใจดีจริงจริง You are really kind.

'Jing (jing) lĕ(r)?' จริง(จริง) เหรอ? is a question equivalent to 'really?' To answer yes, repeat the word 'jing jing'. To answer no, say 'bplàh-oo' เปล่า.

2. 'lĕ(r)?' เหรอ? is a question word that appears at the end of a sentence. It is similar to 'châi mái?' ใช่มั้ย? Both words are used when you want an assurance from the other party. It is similar to 'aren't you?', 'don't you?' To answer yes, say 'châi' ใช่. To answer no, say 'bplàh-oo' เปล่า.

    Ex. Glòht lĕ(r)?
        โกรธเหรอ? You are angry, aren't you?

    Apply 'lĕ(r)?' เหรอ? when the question is negative.
    Ex. Mâi châwp lĕ(r)?
        ไม่ชอบเหรอ? Don't you like it?
    Ex. Mâi ao lĕ(r)?
        ไม่เอาเหรอ? Don't you want it?

3. 'Yahng mâi' ยังไม่ + verb / modifier + le(r)-ii เลย (*not yet*....) 'Le(r)-ii เลย' here acts like an intensifier, you may leave it out.

    Ex. Yahng mâi hâh mohng le(r)-ii
        ยังไม่ห้าโมงเลย It is not 5 o'clock yet.
    Ex. Yahng mâi mêut le(r)-ii
        ยังไม่มืดเลย It is not dark yet.
    Ex. Yahng mâi dii le(r)-ii
        ยังไม่ดีเลย It is not good yet.

4. 'Ge(r)n bpai' เกินไป, when put after adjective or adverb, means too much..., over....

    Ex. Pèht ge(r)n bpai.
        เผ็ดเกินไป Too spicy.
    Ex. Ráwn ge(r)n bpai.
        ร้อนเกินไป Too hot.
    Ex. Dèuk ge(r)n bpai.
        ดึกเกินไป Too late (at night).

⁵ 'Hăh mâi je(r)' หาไม่เจอ is one of the most widely used idioms. 'Hăh' หา means 'to look for'. 'Je(r)' เจอ means 'to meet', 'to find'. This idiom literally means 'you looked for it but couldn't find it.'
Ex. Koon hăh nge(r)n je(r) mái?
คุณหาเงินเจอมั้ย? Did you find your money?
To answer yes = 'je(r)' เจอ
To answer no = 'mâi je(r)' ไม่เจอ

Other useful idioms are:
'Mawng mâi hĕhn' มองไม่เห็น. 'Mawng', มอง means 'to look at'. 'Hĕhn' เห็น means 'to see visually'. 'Mawng mâi hĕhn' มองไม่เห็น means 'can't see'.
Ex. Káo yeun yòo glai mâhk, pŏhm mawng mâi hĕhn káo.
เค้ายืนอยู่ไกลมาก ผมมองไม่เห็นเค้า He is standing so far away, I can't see him.

'Nawn mâi làhp' นอนไม่หลับ. 'Nawn' นอน means to lie down and 'làhp' หลับ means 'to fall asleep'. 'Nawn mâi làhp' นอนไม่หลับ means 'couldn't sleep' or 'can't sleep'.
Ex. Mêua keun níi koon nawn làhp mái?
เมื่อคืนนี้คุณนอนหลับมั้ย? Could you sleep (did you fall asleep) last night?
To answer yes = 'nawn làhp' นอนหลับ
To answer no = 'nawn mâi làhp' นอนไม่หลับ

'Mâi dâi yin' ไม่ได้ยิน, 'dâi yin' ได้ยิน means to hear and 'mâi dâi yin' ไม่ได้ยิน means 'didn't hear', 'can't hear'
Ex. Koon dâi yin pŏhm mái?
คุณได้ยินผมมั้ย? Can you hear me?
To answer yes = 'dâi yin' ได้ยิน
To answer no = 'mâi dâi yin' ไม่ได้ยิน

DRILLS

1. Practice 'Mâi___lĕ(r)?' ไม่___เหรอ? by completing the phrase using the following words.

y<u>á</u>hp	ยับ	wrinkle (clothes)
rîap ráw-ii	เรียบร้อย	tidy, neat
nawn	นอน	to lie down/sleep
n<u>â</u>hng	นั่ง	to sit
róo	รู้	to know
l<u>ê</u>hn	เล่น	to play

2. Practice 'y<u>a</u>hng mâi___' ยังไม่___ by completing the phrase using the following words.

hĭw	หิว	hungry
ìm	อิ่ม	full
paw	พอ	enough
dii	ดี	good (quality)
g<u>è</u>hng	เก่ง	good (skillful)
mâi	ไหม้	to be burnt

EXERCISES

1. How do you say the following sentences in Thai?
    A. This food is too spicy.
    B. The weather here is too hot.
    C. There are too many people.
    D. Really?
    E. It's really far.
    F. Things here are really expensive.
    G. I think it is going to rain.
    H. I know that tomorrow is a holiday.

2. Translate the following sentences into English.
   A. Dâi yin mái? Káo pôot arai?
   ได้ยินมั้ยเค้าพูดอะไร?
   B. Pŏhm hăh gràh bpăo nge(r)n mâi je(r).
   ผมหากระเป๋าเงินไม่เจอ
   C. Mêua wahn níi koon hĕhn káo mái?
   เมื่อวานนี้คุณเห็นเค้ามั้ย?
   D. Mêua keun níi nawn mâi làhp.
   เมื่อคืนนี้นอนไม่หลับ
   E. Mêua gíi níi koon mâi je(r) káo lĕ(r)?
   เมื่อกี้นี้คุณไม่เจอเค้าเหรอ?
   F. Pŏhm bèua jing jing.
   ผมเบื่อจริงๆ
   G. Bpìt ae hâi nàw-ii.
   ปิดแอร์ให้หน่อย
   H. Cháhn róo wâh koon yàhk bpai tîaw.
   ฉันรู้ว่าคุณอยากไปเที่ยว

Appearance is very important in Thailand, and as such, it is not a surprise that the country is becoming a global center for cosmetic surgery. People are generally prejudged by their looks, clothes, jewelry, automobile, etc.

For women, a white complexion is considered beautiful and signifies high status. Skin whitening substances are to be found in most cosmetic products. It is so popular that to find non-whitening cream is difficult. Keeping out of the sun is vital. On a clear day, it is not hard to see Thai women carrying umbrellas out-doors. At the beach, you may see Thai people playing in the sea wearing long trousers and long-sleeved shirts.

14. Grooming

VOCABULARY

tahm pŏhm	ทำผม	to have one's hair set
sàh pŏhm	สระผม	to shampoo
nûat pŏhm	นวดผม	to apply conditioner
dtàht pŏhm	ตัดผม	to have one's hair cut
dàht pŏhm	ดัดผม	to have one's hair waved
saw-ii pŏhm	ซอยผม	to have one's hair feathered
bpào pŏhm	เป่าผม	to have one's hair blow dried
dai pŏhm	ไดร์ผม	to have one's hair blow dried in style
tahm sĭi	ทำสี	to have one's hair colored
pŏhm sâhn	ผมสั้น	short hair
pŏhm yah-oo	ผมยาว	long hair
pŏhm yah-oo bpahn glahng	ผมยาวปานกลาง	medium length hair
kâhng nâh	ข้างหน้า	at the front side
kâhng lăhng	ข้างหลัง	at the back side
kâhng kâhng	ข้างข้าง	at the side
gohn	โกน	to shave
nùat	หนวด	moustache
tahm léhp meu	ทำเล็บมือ	to have a manicure
tahm léhp táh-oo	ทำเล็บเท้า	to have a pedicure
tah léhp	ทาเล็บ	to have one's nails painted
dtâwng	ต้อง	must, have to
kráhng nâh	ครั้งหน้า	next time

tâo náhn	เท่านั้น	only, just
dûay	ด้วย	also, as well[1]
gàwn	ก่อน	preceding, in advance, before[2]
àwk	ออก	out[3]
gwàh	กว่า	more
dii gwàh	ดีกว่า	better
tîi soòt	ที่สุด	the most...
paw dii	พอดี	just fine, the right amount[4]
oh gàht	โอกาส	opportunity, chance
mài	ใหม่	new, again[5]

DIALOGUE

A: Sàh wàht dii kàh. Tahm arai[6] dii káh?
สวัสดีค่ะ ทำอะไรดีคะ? Hello. What can I do for you?

B: Dtàht pŏhm nàw-ii kráhp.
ตัดผมหน่อยครับ I would like to have my hair cut please.

A: Sàh dûay mái káh?
สระด้วยมั้ยคะ? Would you like to shampoo as well?

B: Mâi sàh kráhp.
ไม่สระครับ No.

A: Che(r)n nâhng raw tîi nîi gàwn kàh.
เชิญนั่งรอที่นี่ก่อนค่ะ Please have a seat here first.

B: Dtâwng raw nahn mái kráhp?
ต้องรอนานมั้ยครับ? Do I have to wait long?

A: Mâi nahn kàh, bpràh mahn sìp nah tii tâo náhn.
ไม่นานค่ะ ประมาณสิบนาทีเท่านั้น No, only about 10 minutes.

A: Che(r)n tahng níi kàh.
เชิญทางนี้ค่ะ This way, please.

B: Chûay dtàht kâhng lăhng àwk bpràh mahn nèung níw, láew gâw saw-ii kâhng nâh àwk nít nàw-ii kráhp.
ช่วยตัดข้างหลังออกประมาณหนึ่งนิ้ว แล้วก็ซอยข้างหน้าออกนิดหน่อยครับ
Could you cut the back out 1 inch, and feather the front part a little bit?

A: Tahm sĭi dûay mái káh? Pŏhm kăh-oo yé(r) ler-ii[7].
ทำสีด้วยมั้ยคะ? ผมขาวเยอะเลย Would you like to have your hair dyed as well? You have a lot of gray hair.

B: Ao wái[8] kráhng nâh dii gwàh kráhp. Wahn níi pŏhm mâi mii weh lah mâhk.
เอาไว้ครั้งหน้าดีกว่าครับ วันนี้ผมไม่มีเวลามาก I rather have it done next time. Today I don't have much time.

A: Dâi kàh... Sèht láew kàh.
ได้ค่ะ... เสร็จแล้วค่ะ That's OK... It's done now.

B: Chûay saw-ii kâhng nâh ìik nít nàw-ii dâi mái kráhp?
ช่วยซอยข้างหน้าอีกนิดหน่อยได้มั้ยครับ? Could you feather the front part out a little bit more?

A: Dâi kàh..
ได้ค่ะ Yes, I could.

B: Paw dii láew kráhp... Tâo rai kráhp?
พอดีแล้วครับ... เท่าไรครับ? It's good now... How much is it?

A: Săwng ráw-ii bàht kàh. Oh gàht nâh che(r)n mài náh káh.
สองร้อยบาทค่ะ โอกาสหน้าเชิญใหม่นะคะ It's 200 baht. Please visit us again next time.

GRAMMAR NOTES

[1] 'Dûay' ด้วย meaning 'as well, together' is usually put behind a verb or an object, if any.

Ex. Kăw náhm nèung kùat, láew gâw náhm kăeng dûay.
ขอน้ำหนึ่งขวดแล้วก็น้ำแข็งด้วย May I have a bottle of water and ice as well?

Ex. Koon mâe jàh bpai gàhp koon pâw dûay.
คุณแม่จะไปกับคุณพ่อด้วย Mother will also go with father.

2 'Gàwn' ก่อน, when used in a compound word, it usually indicates past tense, e.g. mêua gàwn níi เมื่อก่อนนี้ (*yesterday*). When it functions as a preposition, it means 'ahead of' or 'preceding'.

Ex. Dì cháhn gin gàwn náh káh.
ดิฉันกินก่อนนะคะ I'll eat first (before you), OK?

Ex. Koon bpai gàwn, dĭaw di cháhn (kâw-ii) dtahm bpai.
คุณไปก่อนเดี๋ยวดิฉัน(ค่อย)ตามไป Please go ahead, I will follow later.

When it functions as a conjunction, it shows an order of events. In this circumstance, it is equivalent to 'before' in English.

Ex. Dì cháhn àhp náhm gáwn bpai tahm ngahn.
ดิฉันอาบน้ำก่อนไปทำงาน I take a bath before I go to work.

Ex. Dì cháhn châwp sùat mohn gàwn kâo nawn.
ดิฉันชอบสวดมนต์ก่อนเข้านอน I like to chant before I go to bed.

3 'Àwk' ออก usually accompanies another verb. When it is the main verb, it often appears with 'bpai' ไป or 'mah' มา which acts like a helping verb. In that case, the meaning is 'to be out' in English. In many cases, 'àwk' ออก also appears as a second verb.

Ex. Àwk mah, yàh kâo bpai.
ออกมา อย่าเข้าไป Come/Get out, don't go in there.

Ex. Gàe sah-dtík-gê(r) àwk mah jàhk glàwng.
แกะสติกเกอร์ออกมาจากกล่อง Take the sticker out of the box.

Ex. Ao mâi àwk.
เอาไม่ออก Can't get it out.

4   'Paw-dii' พอดี is equivalent to an adequate amount, well-suited, good enough, well-fitted.

Ex. Seûa dtua níi sài paw-dii
เสื้อตัวนี้ใส่พอดี This shirt is well-fitted.

5   'Mài' ใหม่ when placed after a verb, it means 'again' but when placed after a noun, it means 'new'.

Ex. Kĭan mài
เขียนใหม่ Write again.

Ex. Róht mài
รถใหม่ New car.

6   'Tahm arai?' ทำอะไร literally means 'what are you doing?' However, in some circumstances, especially when having 'dii' ดี behind it, it means 'What would you like to have done? (What can I do for you?)' In a restaurant, you may hear a waitress asking 'tahn arai káh?' ทานอะไรคะ? It means 'What would you like to eat?' In some other circumstances, when a friend asks you the same question, she actually wants to know what you are eating.

Ex. Séu arai káh?
ซื้ออะไรคะ? What are you buying? / What would you like to buy?

Ex. Séu arai dii káh?
ซื้ออะไรดีคะ? What would you like to buy?

7 'Yé(r) ler-ii' เยอะเลย is equivalent to 'so many' or 'so much'. The word 'yé(r)' เยอะ usually appears after a verb or a noun. 'Ler-ii' เลย here acts as an intensifier of 'yé(r)' เยอะ.
   Ex. Tîi-nîi mii kăwng yé(r) ler-ii.
   ที่นี่มีของเยอะเลย There are a lot of things here.

However, when 'ler-ii' เลย is used in a negative sentence, it means 'at all',
   Ex. Mâi châwp káo ler-ii.
   ไม่ชอบเค้าเลย I don't like him at all.

8 'Ao wái' เอาไว้ often appears with 'kráhng nâh' ครั้งหน้า (*next time*.) Use this combination when you want to put off an activity to another time. You may replace 'kráhng nâh' ครั้งหน้า with 'tii lăhng' ทีหลัง or 'wahn lăhng' วันหลัง when you do not want to specify the exact time. In this case, the final particle 'náh káh' นะคะ or 'náh kráhp' นะครับ (*OK?*) is often added to soften the statement.

DRILLS

1. Practice '__A__ gàwn ก่อน __B__'. __A__ *before* __B__. by completing the phrase using the following words.

   | A. bpraeng fahn | แปรงฟัน | brush teeth |
   | B. àwk jàhk bâhn | ออกจากบ้าน | leave home |

   | A. sàh pŏhm | สระผม | shampoo |
   | B. nûat pŏhm | นวดผม | put on conditioner |

   | A. láhng meu | ล้างมือ | wash hands |
   | B. tahn ah hăhn | ทานอาหาร | eat |

   | A. tahm gahn bâhn | ทำการบ้าน | do homework |
   | B. lêhn kâhng nâwk | เล่นข้างนอก | play outside |

A. sáhk pâh   ซักผ้า   do laundry
B. rîit pâh   รีดผ้า   iron clothes

2. Practice 'Rao jàh bpai ____ gáhp káo dûay' เราจะไป____กับเค้าด้วย *We will go____with him too.* by completing the sentence using the following words.

dtàhng jahng wàht   ต่างจังหวัด   the provinces
yîam nah-ii   เยี่ยมนาย   visit the boss
tah leh   ทะเล   sea
tahm boon   ทำบุญ   make merit
tahm tóo-ráh   ทำธุระ   run an errand

3. Practice 'Groong têhp____gwàh chiang mài' กรุงเทพ____กว่าเชียงใหม่ *Bangkok is____than Chiang Mai.* by completing the sentence using the following words.

glai   ไกล   far
glâi   ใกล้   near
năh-oo   หนาว   cold
ráwn   ร้อน   hot
léhk   เล็ก   small
yài   ใหญ่   big
paeng   แพง   expensive
tòok   ถูก   cheap

EXERCISES

1. How do you say the following sentences in Thai?
    A. I am not hungry at all.
    B. He is not tired at all.

C. Get the pen out of the box.
D. I will read it next time.
E. She has a new friend.
F. Say that again.
G. This shirt fits well.
H. I like swimming the best.
I. Which table do you like more?

2. Please follow the instructions.
   A. Your friends are going to Pattaya. You want to join, so you say...
   B. Your height is 170 cm. Your younger brother is 160 cm. Your older sister is 172 cm. Please make a comparison by using the words 'gwàh' กว่า and 'tîi-sòot' ที่สุด.
   C. You are buying a bottle of water. The shopkeeper gives you a damaged bottle. Ask for a new one.
   D. You are looking for a refrigerator. Please ask to see the best one.
   E. You want to have your hair dyed. At the salon, a Thai person asks you 'Tahm arai káh?' ทำอะไรคะ? Please respond.
   F. You are about to go out to a restaurant, please ask your friend if he wants to join.
   G. You are sitting with your guests at the dining table at home. Please invite your guests to start the meal.
   H. Your friend asks you if you want to go to the movies. Please ask for a raincheck.

At private hospitals, you can make an appointment with a doctor on a short notice or sometimes this is not required at all. Most doctors in well-known private hospitals are able to speak English. Several big hospital chains are trying very hard to promote their services in overseas markets. Claiming their international standards with relatively low prices and no waiting lists, Thailand is becoming a well-known place for medical tourism.

Thai doctors are sometimes rather liberal in the types and quantities of medicine they prescribe, even for relatively minor illnesses. Antibiotics are widely and frequently prescribed. It is not uncommon to get a load of medicines for a minor cold. For small problems, it is possible to seek advice and purchase the appropriate medicine from a pharmacy without a prescription.

15. Medicine

VOCABULARY

yah	ยา	medicine
yah náhm	ยาน้ำ	liquid medicine
yah m<u>é</u>ht	ยาเม็ด	tablet medicine
yah tah	ยาทา	ointment
yah gâe...	ยาแก้...	medicine for...
páe yah	แพ้ยา	allergic to medicine
ráhn kăh-ii yah	ร้านขายยา	drug store
mâi s<u>à</u>h bah-ii	ไม่สบาย	sick
bpùay	ป่วย	sick
bpai hăh	ไปหา	to visit (out-going)
mah hăh	มาหา	to visit (in-coming)
k<u>oh</u>n kâi	คนไข้	patient
măw	หมอ	doctor
peh s<u>à</u>ht ch<u>a</u>h gawn	เภสัชกร	pharmacist
p<u>ah</u> yah bahn	พยาบาล	nurse
rohng p<u>ah</u> yah bahn	โรงพยาบาล	hospital
klii nìk	คลีนิค	clinic
j<u>è</u>hp	เจ็บ	pain
j<u>è</u>hp kaw	เจ็บคอ	sore throat
plăe	แผล	wound

133

mii/bp<u>eh</u>n kâi	มี/เป็นไข้	have a fever
bp<u>eh</u>n w<u>à</u>ht	เป็นหวัด	have a cold
ah gahn	อาการ	symptoms, conditions
ai	ไอ	cough
bpùat	ปวด	ache
bpùat hǔa	ปวดหัว	headache
bpùat táwng	ปวดท้อง	stomachache
táwng sǐa	ท้องเสีย	upset stomach
táwng pòok	ท้องผูก	constipation
nèua-ii	เหนื่อย	tired
hǎh-ii jai	หายใจ	to breath
hǎh-ii jai kâo	หายใจเข้า	to inhale
hǎh-ii jai àwk	หายใจออก	to exhale
mâi mii raeng	ไม่มีแรง	no strength
gleun	กลืน	to swallow
l<u>oh</u>ng	ลง	to go down
j<u>ah</u>m bp<u>eh</u>n	จำเป็น	necessary
dii kêun	ดีขึ้น	better (than before)[1]
w<u>áh</u>t	วัด	to measure
weh lah	เวลา	when (conjunction)[2]
tâh	ถ้า	if
t<u>ah</u>m mai	ทำไม	why?
t<u>óo</u>k k<u>oh</u>n	ทุกคน	everybody
p<u>áh</u>k pàwn	พักผ่อน	to rest
gâw le(r)-ii	ก็เลย	so, therefore[3]
râhng gah-ii	ร่างกาย	body
hǔa	หัว	head

p<u>ŏ</u>hm	ผม	hair
hŭa jai	หัวใจ	heart
nâh	หน้า	face
dtah	ตา	eye
kíw	คิ้ว	eye-brow
j<u>àh</u> mòok	จมูก	nose
bpàhk	ปาก	mouth
f<u>ah</u>n	ฟัน	tooth
lín	ลิ้น	tongue
kahng	คาง	chin
hŏo	หู	ear
kaw	คอ	neck
lài	ไหล่	shoulder
dtua	ตัว	body
kăen	แขน	arm
kăh	ขา	leg
meu	มือ	hand
táh-oo	เท้า	foot
níw meu	นิ้วมือ	finger
níw táh-oo	นิ้วเท้า	toe
nâh <u>òh</u>k	หน้าอก	chest
l<u>ăh</u>ng	หลัง	back
táwng	ท้อง	stomach
eh-oo	เอว	waist
s<u>àh</u> pôhk	สะโพก	hip
gr<u>àh</u> dòok	กระดูก	bone
lêuat	เลือด	blood

DIALOGUE

A: Sàh wàht dii kráhp koon măw.
สวัสดีครับคุณหมอ Hello doctor.

B: Sàh wàht dii kàh. Bpehn arai[4] káh?
สวัสดีค่ะ เป็นอะไรคะ? Hello. What is the problem?

A: Bpehn wàht kráhp. Hăh-ii jai mâi àwk, láew gâw bpùat hŭa dûay kráhp.
เป็นหวัดครับ หายใจไม่ออก แล้วก็ปวดหัวด้วยครับ I have a cold. I can't breathe and I also have a headache.

B: Kăw măw wáht kâi nàw-ii kàh. Chûay âh bpàhk nàw-ii kàh.
ขอหมอวัดไข้หน่อยค่ะ ช่วยอ้าปากหน่อยค่ะ May I measure your temperature? Could you open your mouth please?

A: Jèhp kaw mâhk dûay kràhp. Gleun ah hăhn mâi kâw-ii lohng.
เจ็บคอมากด้วยครับ กลืนอาหารไม่ค่อยลง I have a bad sore throat as well. I can't really swallow food.

B: Doo láew, mâi bpehn arai mâhk, bpehn wàht tahm mah dah tâo náhn kàh. Măw jàh hâi yah gâe jèhp kaw, láew gâw yah gâe bpùat bpai tahn tîi bâhn hâh wahn náh káh.
ดูแล้ว, ไม่เป็นอะไรมาก เป็นหวัดธรรมดาเท่านั้นค่ะ หมอจะให้ยาแก้เจ็บคอ แล้วก็ยาแก้ปวดไปทานที่บ้านห้าวันนะคะ I see nothing serious, just a normal cold. I will give you medicine for sore throat and pain killers for taking at home for 5 days, OK?

A: Yah nîi tahn yahng ngai kráhp?
ยานี้ทานยังไงครับ? How do I take these medicines?

B: Yah gâe jèhp kaw, tahn wahn láh[5] săhm kráhng, kráhng láh săwng méht, lăhng ah hăhn. Yah gâe bpùat, tahn weh lah bpùat hŭa, kráhng láh nèung méht. Tâh ah gahn mâi

dii kêun, mah hăh măw mài náh káh.
ยาแก้เจ็บคอ ทานวันละสามครั้ง ครั้งละสองเม็ดหลังอาหาร ยาแก้ปวด ทานเวลาที่ปวดหัวครั้งละหนึ่งเม็ด ถ้าอาการไม่ดีขึ้น มาหาหมอใหม่นะคะ
The medicine for sore throat, take 3 times a day, 2 tablets a time after meals. The pain killer, take 1 tablet when you have a headache. If your condition is not better, please come back to see me again.

A: Kăw yah gâe ai dûay dâi mái kráhp?
ขอยาแก้ไอด้วยได้มั้ยครับ? May I have medicine for coughing too?

B: Dâi kàh. Bpehn yah náhm, tahn nèung cháwn dtóh tóok sìi chûa mohng.
ได้ค่ะ เป็นยาน้ำ ทานหนึ่งช้อนโต๊ะทุกสี่ชั่วโมง Yes. It's liquid. Take 1 table spoon every four hours.

A: Tahm mai wahn níi mâi mii krai[6] chûay tîi klii nìk kráhp?
ทำไมวันนี้ไม่มีใครช่วยที่คลีนิคครับ? Why nobody is here to help (you) today?

B: Wahn níi tóok kohn bpùay, măw gâw le(r)-ii hâi[7] páhk pàwn yòo tîi bâhn.
วันนี้ทุกคนป่วย หมอก็เลยให้พักผ่อนอยู่ที่บ้าน Everyone is sick today, so I let them rest at home.

A: Kàwp koon kráhp, sàh wàht dii kráhp.
ขอบคุณครับ สวัสดีครับ Thank you. Bye.

GRAMMAR NOTES

[1] When comparing two different objects, use 'gwàh' กว่า as explained in the earlier lesson. However, when comparing one object in different times (before & after), use 'kêun' ขึ้น (*up/more*) or 'lohng' ลง (*down/less*) after adjective or adverb.

   Ex. Koon doo sŭay kêun.
        คุณดูสวยขึ้น You look more beautiful (than before).

Ex. K<u>oo</u>n doo pǎwm l<u>oh</u>ng.
  คุณดูผอมลง You look thinner (than before).

2 'Weh lah' เวลา means 'when' as a conjunction and means 'time' as a noun. When it is a conjunction, it is located at the beginning of the sentence or between the two sub-sentences.
  Ex. Weh lah káo mâi s<u>àh</u> bah-ii, káo j<u>àh</u> ngîap mâhk.
    เวลาเค้าไม่สบาย เค้าจะเงียบมาก
    When he is sick, he is very quiet.
  Ex. Káo j<u>àh</u> ngîap mâhk weh lah káo mâi s<u>àh</u> bah-ii.
    เค้าจะเงียบมาก เวลาเค้าไม่สบาย
    He is very quiet when he is sick.

3 'Gâw le(r)-ii' ก็เลย is a conjunction of a cause-effect sentence. It can be used similarly to 'so', 'therefore'. 'Gâw le(r)-ii' ก็เลย appears after the subject of the second sentence. If the subject of the first sentence (cause) is the same as the second sentence (effect), you may omit the second subject. Observe the word order of the following sentences.
  Ex. Fǒhn dt<u>òh</u>k róht gâw le(r)-ii dtìt.
    ฝนตกรถก็เลยติด It is raining; therefore, the traffic is congested.
  Ex. Di ch<u>áh</u>n hǐw gâw ler-ii gin.
    ดิฉันหิวก็เลยกิน I am hungry, therefore, I eat.

4 'Bp<u>eh</u>n arai?' เป็นอะไร? is an idiom used to ask someone what is wrong with him/her. To answer that you are OK, you may say 'mâi dâi bp<u>eh</u>n arai' ไม่ได้เป็นอะไร (*Nothing's wrong.*) If you want to say 'nothing serious', you may say 'mâi dâi bp<u>eh</u>n arai mâhk' ไม่ได้เป็นอะไรมาก

5. The usage of 'láh' ละ (*per*) is also mentioned in the 'Shopping' lesson. It appears after classifiers. Observe the word order in the following examples.
   Ex. Pŏhm àhp náhm w<u>ah</u>n l<u>áh</u> săhm kr<u>áh</u>ng.
   ผมอาบน้ำวันละสามครั้ง I bathe 3 times a day.
   Ex. K<u>oh</u>n tai dâi y<u>òo</u>t p<u>áh</u>k ráwn bpii l<u>áh</u> sìp w<u>ah</u>n.
   คนไทยได้หยุดพักร้อนปีละสิบวัน Thai people get 10 days annual leave.

6. When 'mâi mii' ไม่มี (*not have*) is placed in front of 'krai' ใคร (*who?*), it means 'no one'. The same rule applies to 'arai' อะไร (*what?*) and 'tîi năi' ที่ไหน (*where?*). Thus, 'mâi mii arai' ไม่มีอะไร means 'nothing' and 'mâi mii tîi năi' ไม่มีที่ไหน means 'nowhere'.

7. 'Hâi' ให้ has several meanings. When it acts as a preposition, it means 'for'. When it acts as a verb, it means 'give', 'let', 'allow', 'command', etc. When you make a request, permission or a command, follow this pattern: subject + 'hâi' ให้ + object + to do something.
   Ex. Káo hâi pŏhm y<u>òo</u>t nèung w<u>ah</u>n.
   เค้าให้ผมหยุดหนึ่งวัน He gave me a day off.
   Ex. Nah-ii hâi pŏhm mah r<u>áh</u>p j<u>òh</u>t m<u>ăh</u>-ii.
   นายให้ผมมารับจดหมาย The boss asked me to come and pick up a letter.

DRILLS

1. Practice 'Weh lah káo __A__ , káo j<u>àh</u> __B__ ' เวลาเค้า __A__ , เค้าจะ __B__ .
   When he/she __A__ , he/she will __B__.
   by completing the sentence using the following words.

   A. ah r<u>oh</u>m dii   อารมณ์ดี   good mood

B. jai dii	ใจดี	kind
A. ah rohm sĭa	อารมณ์เสีย	bad mood
B. nâh glua	น่ากลัว	scary
A. nèua-ii	เหนื่อย	tired
B. ngòot ngìt	หงุดหงิด	frustrated
A. sĭa jai	เสียใจ	sad
B. ráwng hâh-ii	ร้องไห้	cry
A. dii jai	ดีใจ	glad
B. yím	ยิ้ม	smile
A. bpai tîaw	ไปเที่ยว	go out
B. bpai kohn diaw	ไปคนเดียว	go alone
A. tahm ngahn	ทำงาน	work
B. dtâhng jai	ตั้งใจ	pay attention

2. Practice 'Káo __A__, gâw le(r)-ii __B__' เค้า __A__, ก็เลย __B__. He/she is __A__, therefore, he/she __B__.
by completing the sentence using the following words.

A. yôong	ยุ่ง	busy
B. mâi mah	ไม่มา	didn't come
A. ngûang nawn	ง่วงนอน	sleepy
B. bpai nawn	ไปนอน	go to sleep
A. gèhng	เก่ง	skillful
B. mii ngahn mâhk	มีงานมาก	have lots of work
A. kîi gìat	ขี้เกียจ	lazy
B. mâi tahm ngahn	ไม่ทำงาน	doesn't work
A. châwp pèht	ชอบเผ็ด	like it spicy
B. sài prík	ใส่พริก	put chillies in
A. yàhk păwm	อยากผอม	want to be thin
B. wîng tóok wahn	วิ่งทุกวัน	run everyday
A. bpùay	ป่วย	sick, unwell
B. bpai hăh măw	ไปหาหมอ	visit a doctor

EXERCISES

1. Use the word 'gâw le(r)-ii' ก็เลย to conjunct the following sentences.
    A. He is cold. He turns off the air-conditioner.
    B. She is hot. She turns on the air-conditioner.
    C. We are tired. We take a day off.
    D. The room is dark. I turn the light on.
    E. I had a meeting. I had to wake up early.
    F. The radio (wìt ta yóo) วิทยุ was broken. I did not listen to the news.
    G. This bag is not expensive. I want to buy it.
    H. The traffic was very congested. I missed the appointment.
    I. I did not hear the phone ring. I did not answer the phone.

2. How do you say the following sentences in Thai?
    A. How much is this per kilo?
    B. I go there three times a week.
    C. I exercise 45 minutes a time.
    D. He let me go home.
    E. Who let you sit?
    F. He did not ask you to call me.
    G. Nobody's here.
    H. Nowhere is cheap.
    I. Nothing is on the table.

3. Please respond to the following situations in Thai.
   A. You were sick. Now you are better. Someone asks you how you are now.
   B. You see that something is wrong with your friend. Ask him what's wrong.
   C. If there is nothing wrong with him, he would say...
   D. Your friend from Chiangmai is visiting you in Bangkok. Ask him how often he comes to Bangkok by using the word 'l<u>á</u>h' ละ .
   E. You told your friend, Jim, to come and pick up something. Someone else shows up. Please ask that person if he's sent by Jim.
   F. You have been coughing a lot; ask for medicine at a pharmacist.

4. Translate the following sentences into English.
   A. K<u>oo</u>n doo sŭay k<u>ê</u>un. คุณดูสวยขึ้น
   B. Tahn yah w<u>ah</u>n l<u>á</u>h sìi kr<u>á</u>hng. ทานยาวันละสี่ครั้ง
   C. K<u>oo</u>n mâe hâi mah ao n<u>ăh</u>ng sĕu. คุณแม่ให้มาเอาหนังสือ
   D. Weh lah p<u>ŏh</u>m hĭw mâhk, p<u>ŏh</u>m chăwp mah gin tîi nîi.
      เวลาผมหิวมาก ผมชอบมากินที่นี่
   E. Káo mâi yòo tîi n<u>â</u>hn, di ch<u>á</u>hn gâw le(r)-ii mah mâi dâi. เค้าไม่อยู่ที่นั่น ดิฉันก็เลยมาไม่ได้
   F. Mâi mii arai nai gr<u>à</u>h bpăo. ไม่มีอะไรในกระเป๋า
   G. W<u>ah</u>n níi mâi mii krai r<u>á</u>hp toh r<u>a</u>h s<u>à</u>hp.
      วันนี้ไม่มีใครรับโทรศัพท์

Thailand is comparatively a rather safe place to live. However, petty crimes, especially in big cities like Bangkok, Pattaya or Phuket are not uncommon. Most common petty crimes are pickpocketing and 'bag-snatching' from a by-passing motorcycle. Thai criminals usually are not violent when conducting petty crimes. When a crime occurs, you can seek help from police by calling 191 or by reporting to the police in person.

It is wise to first find out which local police station has authority over the area where the crime took place. It is possible that you will experience language barriers when reporting the incident. You can obtain a police report from the police officer on duty, usually without cost. If you are in Thailand on a tourist visa, you may report to the tourist police or call 1155 for help.

16. Petty Crime

VOCABULARY

dt<u>ah</u>m rùat	ตำรวจ	police
jâeng kwahm	แจ้งความ	to report to the police
bai jâeng kwahm	ใบแจ้งความ	police report
k<u>ah</u> moh-ii	ขโมย	steal; burglar, thief
tòok + verb	ถูก...	passive voice; to be...[1]
gè(r)t arai k<u>êu</u>n?	เกิดอะไรขึ้น	What happened?
lâo	เล่า	to tell (story)[2]
rah-ii l<u>áh</u> ìat	รายละเอียด	details
doo kăwng	ดูของ	window shopping
ch<u>oh</u>n	ชน	to bump
hăhn	หัน	to turn (your body)
dtawn	ตอน	when (conj.)
dtawn râek	ตอนแรก	at first
dtawn l<u>ăh</u>ng	ตอนหลัง	later
pê(r)ng j<u>àh</u> + verb	เพิ่งจะ...	just...
ao + something + bpai	เอา...ไป	take something away
hăh-ii	หาย	lost (adj.)[3]
bp<u>ah</u>n hăh	ปัญหา	problem
nge(r)n	เงิน	money
nge(r)n s<u>òh</u>t	เงินสด	cash
b<u>àh</u>t kreh dìt	บัตรเครดิต	credit card

bai k<u>à</u>hp kìi	ใบขับขี่	driver's license
g<u>oo</u>n jae	กุญแจ	key
g<u>oo</u>n jae bâhn	กุญแจบ้าน	house key
g<u>oo</u>n jae r<u>ó</u>ht	กุญแจรถ	car key
èun	อื่น	other
yàhng èun	อย่างอื่น	other things
gr<u>àh</u> bpăo	กระเป๋า	handbag
t<u>ŏo</u>ng	ถุง	plastic/paper bag
j<u>òh</u>t	จด	to make note, write
b<u>ah</u>n t<u>éuk</u>	บันทึก	a note, a record
rah-ii ngahn	รายงาน	report
bpr<u>àh</u> j<u>ah</u>m w<u>ahn</u>	ประจำวัน	daily
gr<u>àh</u> bpăo nge(r)n	กระเป๋าเงิน	wallet
dtìt dtàw	ติดต่อ	to contact
pr<u>áw</u> wâh	เพราะว่า	because
hăh	หา	to find
je(r)/p<u>óh</u>p	เจอ/พบ	to meet
hăh...mâi je(r)	หา...ไม่เจอ	can't find...
g<u>èh</u>p (something)+ wái	เก็บ...ไว้	to keep (in a safe place)[4]
dt<u>òh</u>k jai	ตกใจ	shock
jai y<u>eh</u>n y<u>eh</u>n	ใจเย็นๆ	take it easy, calm down
rôop râhng	รูปร่าง	figure, shape
sŏong	สูง	tall
dtîa	เตี้ย	short
ûan	อ้วน	fat
păwm	ผอม	thin

DIALOGUE

A: Sàh wàht dii kráhp. Mii arai hâi chûay mái kráhp?
  สวัสดีครับ มีอะไรให้ช่วยมั้ยครับ? Hello. Anything I can do for you?

B: Sàh wàht dii kàh. Di cháhn mah jâeng kwahm gràh bpăo nge(r)n tòok kah moh-ii kàh.
  สวัสดีค่ะ ดิฉันมาแจ้งความกระเป๋าเงินถูกขโมยค่ะ Hello. I have come to report that my wallet was stolen.

A: Tîi năi kráhp?
  ที่ไหนครับ? Where?

B: Tîi dtàh làht jàh dtòo jàhk kàh.
  ที่ตลาดจตุจักรค่ะ At Jatujak market.

A: Hăh-ii dtawn gìi mohng kráhp?
  หายตอนกี่โมงครับ? What time did you lose it?

B: Bpràh mahn tîang kàh.
  ประมาณเที่ยงค่ะ Around noon.

A: Gè(r)t arai kêun kráhp? Chûay lâo rah-ii láh iat nàw-ii kráhp.
  เกิดอะไรขึ้นครับ ช่วยเล่ารายละเอียดหน่อยครับ What happened? Could you tell me in detail?

B: Dtawn di cháhn gahm lahng de(r)n doo kăwng yòo, róo sèuk wâh mii kohn de(r)n mah chohn, gâw le(r)-ii hăhn bpai doo. Hĕhn pôo chah-ii wîng bpai tahng kâhng lăhng. Dtawn râek, mâi róo wâh gràh bpăo nge(r)n hăh-ii. Dtawn lăhng, pê(r)ng jàh róo práw wâh yàhk séu kăwng, dtàe hăh gràh bpăo nge(r)n mâi je(r).
  ตอนดิฉันกำลังเดินดูของอยู่ รู้สึกว่ามีคนเดินมาชน ก็เลยหันไปดู เห็น
  ผู้ชายวิ่งไปทางข้างหลัง ตอนแรกไม่รู้ว่ากระเป๋าเงินหาย ตอนหลังเพิ่ง
  จะรู้ เพราะว่าอยากซื้อของแต่หากระเป๋าเงินไม่เจอ
  While I was window-shopping, I felt someone bump into me, so I turned to look. I saw a man running to the back.

At first I didn't know that my wallet was gone. I just realized later because I wanted to buy things but I couldn't find the wallet.

A: Jahm dâi mái wâh pôo chah-ii kohn náhn mii rôop râhng yahng ngai⁵?
จำได้มั้ย ว่าผู้ชายคนนั้นมีรูปร่างยังไง? Do you remember what that man looked like?

B: Sŏong, păwm, sài sêua sĭi dahm, ah yóo bpràh mahn yîi sìp bpii kàh.
สูง ผอม ใส่เสื้อสีดำ อายุประมาณยี่สิบปีค่ะ He was tall, thin, wore a black shirt and was about 20 years old.

A: Mii arai hăh-ii bâhng kráhp?
มีอะไรหายบ้างครับ? What did you lose?

B: Nge(r)n sòht săwng pahn bàht, láew gâw bàht wii sâh gàhp bai kàhp kìi kàh.
เงินสดสองพันบาท แล้วก็บัตรวีซ่ากับใบขับขี่ค่ะ 2,000 baht cash and a visa card and a driver's license.

A: Mii yàhng èun⁶ mái kráhp?
มีอย่างอื่นมั้ยครับ? Was there anything else?

B: Kít wâh mâi mii kàh.
คิดว่าไม่มีค่ะ I don't think so.

A: Pŏhm jàh jòht bahn téuk wái nai rah-ii ngahn bpràh jahm wahn náh kráhp.
ผมจะจดบันทึกไว้ในรายงานประจำวันนะครับ I will note it down in the daily report.

B: Di cháhn kăw bai jâeng kwahm gèpt wái bpehn làhk tăhn dûay kàh.
ดิฉันขอใบแจ้งความเก็บไว้เป็นหลักฐานด้วยค่ะ I would like to have a police report to keep as evidence.

GRAMMAR NOTES

1. Thais do not use the passive voice as widely as in English. The passive voice is generally used in Thai only when referring to events of a violent or unpleasant nature such as 'kàh' moh-ii' ขโมย (*steal*), 'dtii' ตี (*hit*), 'chohn' ชน (*bump*), 'wâh' ว่า (*scold*), 'tahm tôht' ทำโทษ (*punish*), etc. When used, it is denoted by the addition of the word 'tòok' ถูก in front of the verb.

   Structure: Subject + 'tòok' ถูก + object (if any) + verb.

   Ex. Káo tòok koon mâe tahm tóht.
   เค้าถูกคุณแม่ทำโทษ He was punished by his mother.

   Ex. Pŏhm tòok nah-ii wâh.
   ผมถูกนายว่า I was scolded by my boss.

2. 'Lâo' เล่า means 'to tell', 'to say'. It is usually used for telling a story. Observe the following two structures:

   1. lâo เล่า + wâh ว่า +...
   Ex. Káo lâo wâh fŏhn dtòhk nàhk mâhk.
   เค้าเล่าว่าฝนตกหนักมาก He said it rained very hard.

   2. lâo เล่า + hâi ให้ + someone + fahng wâh ฟังว่า
   Ex. Káo lâo hâi pŏhm fahng wâh fŏhn dtòhk nàhk mâhk.
   เค้าเล่าให้ผมฟังว่าฝนตกหนักมาก He told me that it rained very hard.

3. 'Hăh-ii' หาย in this context is similar to 'lost'. It acts as an adjective. If you want to use it as a verb 'to lose something'; say 'tahm ทำ + something + hăh-ii' หาย. If you lose your way, use 'lŏhng tahng' หลงทาง instead.

   Ex. Di cháhn tahm nah lí gah hăh-ii.
   ดิฉันทำนาฬิกาหาย I lost my watch.

Ex. Nah lí gah di cháhn hăh-ii.
   นาฬิกาดิฉันหาย My watch is lost.

The same rules apply to the following verbs; dtàek แตก (*broken into little pieces*), hàhk หัก (*broken into a few pieces*), sĭa เสีย (*out-of-order, spoiled*).

Ex. Gâo îi hàhk.
   เก้าอี้หัก The chair is broken.

Ex. Káo tahm gâo îi hàhk.
   เค้าทำเก้าอี้หัก He broke the chair.

4 'Gèhp' เก็บ means 'to pick up', 'to keep'. Observe the following structure:
'Gèhp' เก็บ + object (sometimes omitted) + 'wái' ไว้.
Ex. Gèhp bpàhk gah wái nai lín cháhk.
เก็บปากกาไว้ในลิ้นชัก Keep the pen in the drawer.

Ex. Koon gèhp rawng táo di cháhn wái tîi năi?
   คุณเก็บรองเท้าดิฉันไว้ที่ไหน?
   Where did you keep (put) my shoes?

'Wái' ไว้ often accompanies verbs like 'wahng' วาง (*to place*), 'sài' ใส่ (*to put on/in*), 'tĕu' ถือ (*to hold/carry*). When it appears as a second verb, it indicates that 'the object' is being kept well.

Ex. Sài mùak wái, yàh tàwt.
   ใส่หมวกไว้อย่าถอด Keep the hat on, don't take it off.

Ex. Tĕu gràh bpăo wái nâen nâen.
   ถือกระเป๋าไว้แน่นๆ Hold the bag tight.

5 When inquiring about someone's appearance, you may say 'mii rôop râhng yahng ngai?' มีรูปร่างยังไง? for one's figure and 'mii nâh dtah yahng ngai?' มีหน้าตายังไง? for one's facial look.

6. 'Èun' อื่น means 'other' or 'another', depending on the context. It appears after a classifier.

   Ex. Mii róht kahn èun mái? Di cháhn mâi châwp kahn níi.
   มีรถคันอื่นมั้ย ดิฉันไม่ชอบคันนี้ Do you have another car? I don't like this one.

   Ex. Náhm kùat níi bpè(r)t láew, kùat èun yahng mâi bpè(r)t.
   น้ำขวดนี้เปิดแล้ว ขวดอื่นยังไม่เปิด This bottle of water is already opened. The other bottles are not yet opened.

DRILLS

1. Practice ' Káo tòok A   B ' เค้าถูก A B. *He was B by A.* by completing the sentence using the following words.

A. john	โจร	robber
B. bplôhn	ปล้น	rob
A. pêuan	เพื่อน	friend
B. dtii	ตี	hit
A. ahn tah pahn	อันธพาล	hooligan
B. tahm ráh-ii	ทำร้าย	hurt
A. kroo	ครู	teacher
B. tahm tôht	ทำโทษ	punish
A. sàht dtroo	ศัตรู	enemy
B. johm dtii	โจมตี	attack

2. Change pattern 1 into pattern 2. See the following examples.
   1. Jahn dtáek.
      จานแตก The plate is broken into little pieces.
   2. Káo tahm jahn dtàek.
      เค้าทำจานแตก He broke the plate.

A. Róht sǐa. รถเสีย The car is broken.
B. Toh rah sàhp sǐa. โทรศัพท์เสีย The telephone is broken.
C. Gâew dtàek. แก้วแตก The glass is broken.
D. Kùat dtàek. ขวดแตก The bottle is broken.
E. Mái bahn táht hàhk. ไม้บรรทัดหัก The ruler is broken.
F. Kǎh dtóh hàhk. ขาโต๊ะหัก The table's leg is broken.
G. Nah li gah hǎh-ii. นาฬิกาหาย The watch is lost.
H. Glâwng hǎh-ii. กล้องหาย The camera is lost.

EXERCISES

1. Say the following sentences in Thai, using the words given in the brackets.
   A. He told me that yesterday he saw you. (lâo) เล่า
   B. Do you have another bottle? (èun) อื่น
   C. Keep that paper on the desk. (gèhp..wái) เก็บ..ไว้
   D. Do you know where he keeps his key? (gèhp..wái) เก็บ..ไว้
   E. We lost the way. (lǒhng) หลง
   F. You broke the telephone. (tahm..sǐa) ทำ..เสีย
   G. He got robbed. (tòok) ถูก
   H. The plate is broken. (dtàek) แตก

2. Translate the following sentences into English.
   A. Káo sǒong mâhk. เค้าสูงมาก
   B. Kǎo ûan dtîa. เค้าอ้วนเตี้ย
   C. Pǒhm yah-oo, sài sêua sǐi daeng. ผมยาวใส่เสื้อสีแดง
   D. Pôo yǐng pǎwm, sài rawng táh-oo sǐi dahm. ผู้หญิงผอม ใส่รองเท้าสีดำ

E. Pôo chah-ii dtîa, mâi ûan, mâi pǎwm. ผู้ชายเตี้ย ไม่อ้วน ไม่ผอม

F. K<u>oh</u>n mii ah yóo bpr<u>à</u>h mahn sìi sìp gwàh bpii. คนมีอายุประมาณสี่สิบกว่าปี

G. Mâi dtîa, mâi sŏong mâhk. ไม่เตี้ย ไม่สูงมาก

H. Mâi gàe mâhk. ไม่แก่มาก

17. Key to Exercises

1. PHONETICS

1) A2, B2, C1, D1, E2, F2, G1, H1, I1, J1, K2, L2, M2

2) A. làw หล่อ (*handsome*) B. nâh หน้า (*face, front*)
   C. glai ไกล (*far*) D. glâi ใกล้ (*near*)
   E. glua กลัว (*afraid*) F. hǐw หิว (*hungry*)
   G. dàh ด่า (*to scold*) H. gâew แก้ว (*glass*)
   I. jahm จำ (*to memorize*) J. jai ใจ (*heart, mind*)
   K. bâhn บ้าน (*house*) L. rian เรียน (*to study*)
   M. nèua-ii เหนื่อย (*tired*) N. náht นัด (*appointment*)
   O. mêut มืด (*dark*) P. náhm น้ำ (*water*)
   Q. hâwng ห้อง (*room*) R. kít คิด (*to think*)
   S. leum ลืม (*to forget*) T. kàhp ขับ (*to drive*)
   U. nǎhng หนัง (*movie*) V. nawn นอน (*to sleep*)
   W. lêhn เล่น (*to play*) X. ráh-ii ร้าย (*bad*)
   Y. sǐi สี (*color*) Z. hâh ห้า (*five*)

2. GRAMMAR INTRODUCTION

1) A. Bâhn (kǎwng) káo บ้าน(ของ)เค้า
   B. Bâhn (kǎwng) káo yài บ้าน(ของ)เค้าใหญ่
   C. Bâhn (kǎwng) káo yài mái? บ้าน(ของ)เค้าใหญ่มั้ย?
   D. Cháhn/pǒhm hěhn koon. ฉัน/ผมเห็นคุณ
   E. Koon hěhn arai? คุณเห็นอะไร?
   F. Bpràh têht tai ráwn ประเทศไทยร้อน
   G. Bpràh têht tai mâi nǎh-oo ประเทศไทยไม่หนาว

H. Bpràh têht léhk ประเทศเล็ก
I. Káo bpai tahm ngahn เค้าไปทำงาน
J. Káo bpai tahm ngahn yahng ngai? เค้าไปทำงานยังไง?
K. Pûak káo năh-oo พวกเค้าหนาว
L. Pûak káo mâi ráwn พวกเค้าไม่ร้อน
M. Koon năh-oo mái? คุณหนาวมั้ย?

2) A. We will stay here.   B. Where will you stay?
   C. The weather is hot.   D. The weather here is hot.
   E. Good at one's job.   F. He is good at his job.
   G. He is not good at his job.   H. Go there.
   I. You are going there, aren't you?
   J. Are you going there?   K. Why are you going there?
   L. Who is going there?   M. He/she is there.

3. GREETINGS AND USEFUL PHRASES

1) A. Yin dii kàh/kráhp ยินดีค่ะ/ครับ
      or Mâi bpehn rai kàh/kráhp ไม่เป็นไรค่ะ/ครับ
   B. Mâi bpehn rai kàh/kráhp ไม่เป็นไรค่ะ/ครับ
   C. Sàh wàht dii kàh/kráhp สวัสดีค่ะ/ครับ
   D. Làew je(r) gahn kàh/kráhp แล้วเจอกันค่ะ/ครับ
      or Sàh wàht dii kàh/kráhp สวัสดีค่ะ/ครับ
   E. Sàh wàht dii kàh/kráhp สวัสดีค่ะ/ครับ
      or Làew je(r) gahn kàh/kráhp แล้วเจอกันค่ะ/ครับ.

2) A-3, B-2 or 1, C-1, D-5, E-4.

4. NATIONALITY, FAMILY AND CAREER

1) A. Chêu lêhn arai káh/kráhp? ชื่อเล่นอะไรคะ/ครับ?
   B. Ah yóo tâo rai káh/kráhp? อายุเท่าไรคะ/ครับ?

C. Nahm sàh goon arai káh/kráhp? นามสกุลอะไรคะ/ครับ?
D. Chêu arai káh/kráhp? ชื่ออะไรคะ/ครับ?
E. Tahm ngahn arai káh/ kráhp? ทำงานอะไรคะ/ครับ?
F. Bpehn kohn arai káh/kráhp? เป็นคนอะไรคะ/ครับ?
G. Mah jàhk bpràh têht arai káh/kráhp?
มาจากประเทศอะไรคะ/ครับ?

2) A. Koon châwp arai káh/kráhp? คุณชอบอะไรคะ/ครับ?
B. Baw ri sàht koon yòo tîi năi káh/kráhp?
บริษัทคุณอยู่ที่ไหนคะ/ครับ?
C. Baw ri sàht koon chêu arai káh/kráhp?
บริษัทคุณชื่ออะไรคะ/ครับ?
D. Pahn rah yah koon mah jàhk tîi năi káh/kráhp?
ภรรยาคุณมาจากที่ไหนคะ/ครับ?
E. Náwng chah-ii koon ah yóo tâo rai káh/kráhp?
น้องชายคุณอายุเท่าไรคะ/ครับ?
F. Koon bpehn kohn tai châi mái káh/kráhp?
คุณเป็นคนไทยใช่มั้ยคะ/ครับ?
G. Koon tahm ngahn arai káh/kráhp? คุณทำงานอะไรคะ/ครับ?

5. NUMBERS
1) A. yîi sìp, èht ยี่สิบเอ็ด
B. nèung ráw-ii, hòhk sìp, jèht หนึ่งร้อยหกสิบเจ็ด
C. săwng pahn, jèht ráw-ii, gâh-oo sìp สองพันเจ็ดร้อยเก้าสิบ
D. hâh mèun, hòhk pahn, gâh-oo ráw-ii, bpàet sìp, jèht
ห้าหมื่นหกพันเก้าร้อยแปดสิบเจ็ด
E. săwng săen, săhm mèun, sìi pahn, bpàet sìp, hâh
สองแสนสามหมื่นสี่พันแปดสิบห้า
F. săwng láhn, nèung săen, săhm mèun, hòhk ráw-ii, hâh
sìp สองล้านหนึ่งแสนสามหมื่นหกร้อยห้าสิบ

2) A. 1,400 or 1,004   B. 25,000 or 20,005
   C. 7,080,000   D. 603,000
   E. 16,000   F. 820

6. EATING OUT

1) A. May I have more rice, please?
   B. This fruit is already rotten.
   C. Do you have more ice?
   D. May I have three more cups of tea please?
   E. No MSG please.
   F. What would you like to drink? (What beverage would you like to take?)
   G. Put a little bit of chilli.
   H. Well done, please.
   I. What is delicious here?

2) A. Kăw gah fae y<u>eh</u>n ìik săhm (gâew) k<u>àh</u>/kr<u>áh</u>p. ขอกาแฟเย็นอีกสาม(แก้ว)ค่ะ/ครับ
   B. Ao kâh-oo p<u>àh</u>t sài glàwng gl<u>àh</u>p bâhn เอาข้าวผัดใส่กล่องกลับบ้าน
   C. Ch<u>éh</u>k bin k<u>àh</u>/kr<u>áh</u>p เช็คบิลค่ะ/ครับ
   D. Mâi dtâwng tawn k<u>àh</u>/kr<u>áh</u>p ไม่ต้องทอนค่ะ/ครับ
   E. Ch<u>áh</u>n/p<u>ŏh</u>m mâi dâi s<u>àh</u>ng jahn níi k<u>àh</u>/kr<u>áh</u>p ฉัน/ผมไม่ได้สั่งจานนี้ค่ะ/ครับ
   F. Ao p<u>èh</u>t mâhk k<u>àh</u>/kr<u>áh</u>p. เอาเผ็ดมากค่ะ/ครับ
   G. Chûay yâek bin n<u>àw-ii</u> k<u>àh</u>/kr<u>áh</u>p ช่วยแยกบิลหน่อยค่ะ/ครับ
   H. Kăw meh noo n<u>àw-ii</u> k<u>àh</u>/kr<u>áh</u>p. ขอเมนูหน่อยค่ะ/ครับ
   I. <u>Ah</u> r<u>àw-ii</u> mâhk k<u>àh</u>/kr<u>áh</u>p อร่อยมากค่ะ/ครับ

7. SHOPPING

1) A. Mii sǐi daeng mái/réu bplàh-oo káh/kráhp?
   มีสีแดงมั้ย/รึเปล่าคะ/ครับ?
   B. Tahn/gin mòht mái/réu bplàh-oo káh/kráhp?
   ทาน/กินหมดมั้ย/รึเปล่าคะครับ?
   C. Sèht réu yahng káh/kráhp? เสร็จรึยังคะ/ครับ?
   D. Pǒhm/cháhn yàhk dâi/mii bâhn ผม/ฉันอยากได้/มีบ้าน
   E. Pǒhm/cháhn yàhk lêhn bpian noh ผม/ฉันอยากเล่นเปียนโน
   F. Léhk (ge(r)n) bpai เล็ก(เกิน)ไป
   G. Mii sâhn gwàh níi mái káh/kráhp? มีสั้นกว่านี้มั้ยคะ/ครับ?
   H. Nîi léhk tîi sòot kàh/kráhp นี่เล็กที่สุดค่ะ/ครับ
   I. Pǒhm/ cháhn róo jàhk bahng kohn tîi nîi.
   ผม/ฉันรู้จักบางคนที่นี่
   J. Tǒong táo kôo níi tâo rai káh/kráhp? ถุงเท้าคู่นี้เท่าไรคะ/ครับ?

2) A. Kǎw náhm nèung kùat gàhp chah nèung tûay kàh/kráhp. ขอน้ำหนึ่งขวดกับชาหนึ่งถ้วยค่ะ/ครับ
   B. Sêua (rah kah) dtua láh tâo rai káh/kráhp? เสื้อ(ราคา)ตัวละเท่าไรคะ/ครับ?
   C. Tahn/gin mòht réu bplàh-oo/mái káh/kráhp? ทาน/กินหมดรึเปล่า/มั้ยคะ/ครับ?
   D. Bpràh têht ah meh ri gah yài gwàh bpràh têht tai
   ประเทศอเมริกาใหญ่กว่าประเทศไทย
   Bpràh têht tai yài gwàh bpràh têht sǐng kah bpoh
   ประเทศไทยใหญ่กว่าสิงคโปร์
   Bpràh têht sǐng kah bpoh léhk tîi sòot ประเทศสิงคโปร์เล็กที่สุด
   Or Bpràh têht sǐng kah bpoh léhk gwàh bpràh têht tai
   ประเทศสิงคโปร์เล็กกว่าประเทศไทย
   Bpràh têht tai léhk gwàh bpràh têht ah meh ri gah
   ประเทศไทยเล็กกว่าประเทศอเมริกา

Bpràh têht ah meh ri gah yài tîi sòot
ประเทศอเมริกาใหญ่ที่สุด

E. Ah hăhn tîi bpràh têht ah meh ri gah paeng gwàh tîi bpràh têht tai อาหารที่ประเทศอเมริกาแพงกว่าที่ประเทศไทย

F. Mii (dtua) yài gwàh níi mái káh/kráhp?
มีตัวใหญ่กว่านี้มั้ยคะ/ครับ?

G. Mii sĭi èun mái káh/kráhp? มีสีอื่นมั้ยคะ/ครับ?

H. Lóht dâi mái káh/kráhp? ลดได้มั้ยคะ/ครับ?

I. Séu năhng sĕu pim dâi tîi năi káh/kráhp? ซื้อหนังสือพิมพ์ได้ที่ไหนคะ/ครับ?

J. Dtèuk níi mii gìi kohn? ตึกนี้มีกี่คน? Or mii gìi kohn (yòo) nai dtèuk níi? มีกี่คะ(อยู่)ในตึกนี้?

8. DIRECTIONS

1) A. Tîi nâhn (yòo) glai mái? ที่นั่น(อยู่)ไกลมั้ย?

   B. Mâi bpai tahng dùan ไม่ไปทางด่วน

   C. Kêun táek sîi dâi tîi năi káh/kráhp? ขึ้นแท็กซี่ได้ที่ไหนคะ/ครับ?

   D. Róht fai fáh pàhn rohng pah yah bahn pah yah tai mái káh/kráhp? รถไฟฟ้าผ่านโรงพยาบาลพญาไทมั้ยคะ/ครับ?

   E. Le(r)-ii mah láew kàh/kráhp เลยมาแล้วค่ะ/ครับ Or Pàhn mah láew kàh/kráhp ผ่านมาแล้วค่ะ/ครับ

   F. Chít sáh-ii kàh/kráhp ชิดซ้ายค่ะ/ครับ

   G. Chít kwăh kàh/kráhp ชิดขวาค่ะ/ครับ

   H. Yòo lehn glahng kàh/kráhp อยู่เลนกลางค่ะ/ครับ

   I. Kàhp cháh cháh nàw-ii kàh/kráhp ขับช้าๆ หน่อยค่ะ/ครับ

   J. Jàwt tîi săhn yahn fai kàh/kráhp จอดที่สัญญาณไฟค่ะ/ครับ

2) A. Bpai rohng pah yah bahn bahm roong râht kàh/kráhp
   ไปโรงพยาบาลบำรุงราษฎร์ค่ะ/ครับ

B. Bpai tahng dùan kàh/kráhp ไปทางด่วนค่ะ/ครับ
C. Líaw sáh-ii tîi tahng yâek kàh/ kráhp
เลี้ยวซ้ายที่ทางแยกค่ะ/ครับ
D. Líaw kwăh tîi săhn yahn fai kàh/kráhp เลี้ยวขวาที่สัญญาณไฟค่ะ/ครับ
E. Jàwt tîi sàh pahn law-ii kàh/kráhp จอดที่สะพานลอยค่ะ/ครับ
F. Dtrohng bpai, láew líaw kwăh tîi tahng yâek ตรงไปแล้วเลี้ยวขวาที่ทางแยก
G. Ráhn ah hăhn yòo tahng kwăh ร้านอาหารอยู่ทางขวา
H. Dtèuk yòo kâhng nâh ตึกอยู่ข้างหน้า

3) A. Which station do I get off for Jatujak market?
B. Which bus stop do I get off for Central Chidlom?
C. Do you pass Rama 4 road?
D. Go to the end of the Soi.
E. Cross the road to the other side.
F. Turn right at the third intersection.
G. Go upstairs and turn left.
H. Stop after the bridge.

9. TELLING TIME

1) A. Today at 4 p.m.   B. Tomorrow at 3 a.m.
   C. Yesterday at 1:30 p.m. D. Sunday at 8 p.m.
   E. Friday at 6 p.m.   F. Tuesday at 7 p.m.
   G. 00:40   H. 12:30

2) A. Gìi mohng láew? กี่โมงแล้ว?
   B. Deun arai? เดือนอะไร?
   C. Wahn arai? วันอะไร?

D. Bpii arai? ปีอะไร?
E. Tîang sìi sìp hâh เที่ยงสี่สิบห้า
F. Sìi mohng yehn yîi sìp nah tii สี่โมงเย็นยี่สิบนาที
G. Sìi tôom krêung สี่ทุ่มครึ่ง
H. Dtii sìi sìp nah tii ตีสี่สิบนาที

3) A. Rohng raem hil dtâhn yòo glai kâe nǎi káh/kráhp?
   โรงแรมฮิลตันอยู่ไกลแค่ไหนคะ/ครับ?
   B. Pattaya yòo glai kâe nǎi káh/kráhp?
   พัทยาอยู่ไกลแค่ไหนคะ/ครับ?
   C. Ah hǎhn pèht kâe nǎi káh/kráhp? อาหารเผ็ดแค่ไหนคะ/ครับ?
   D. Bâhn káo yài kâe nǎi káh/kráhp? บ้านเค้าใหญ่แค่ไหนคะ/ครับ?
   E. Tîi tahm ngahn káo léhk kâe nǎi káh/kráhp?
   ที่ทำงานเค้าเล็กแค่ไหนคะ/ครับ?
   F. Ah gàht ráwn kâe nǎi káh/kráhp? อากาศร้อนแค่ไหนคะ/ครับ?
   G. Ah gàht nǎh-oo kâe nǎi káh/kráhp? อากาศหนาวแค่ไหนคะ/ครับ?
   H. Pǒhm káo yah-oo kâe nǎi káh/kráhp? ผมเค้ายาวแค่ไหนคะ/ครับ?

10. APPOINTMENTS

1) A. Please make an appointment with Khun Susan for me
   B. Tell her that we will see each other tomorrow at 10 p.m.
   C. Tell him that Susan cancelled today's appointment.
   D. I thought you would be late.
   E. Is the traffic bad today?
   F. Has he been here long?
   G. Not long.
   H. Approximately 20 minutes.

I. Have you been here before?

J. I have never met him.

2) A. Chûay náht koon Sam hâi nàw-ii kàh/kráhp.
ช่วยนัดคุณแซมให้หน่อยค่ะ/ครับ

B. Chûay náht măw fahn tîi bahm roong râht hâi nàw-ii kàh/kráhp. ช่วยนัดหมอฟันที่บำรุงราษฎร์ให้หน่อยค่ะ/ครับ

C. Kăw tôht kàh/kráhp, cháhn/pŏhm mah săh-ii.
ขอโทษค่ะฉัน/ผมมาสายค่ะ/ครับ

D. Láew je(r) gahn prôong níi kàh/kráhp. แล้วเจอกันพรุ่งนี้ค่ะ/ครับ

E. Je(r) gahn tîi bâhn dtawn hâh mohng. เจอกันที่บ้านตอนห้าโมง

F. Cháhn/pŏhm náht koon Sam wái ฉัน/ผมนัดคุณแซมไว้

G. Cháhn/pŏhm náht káo wái ฉัน/ผมนัดเค้าไว้

H. Náht wái réu yahng káh/kráhp? นัดไว้รึยังคะ/ครับ?

I. Bàwk káo wâh cháhn/pŏhm jàh bpai săh-ii sìp hâh nah tii บอกเค้าว่าฉัน/ผมจะไปสายสิบห้านาที

J. Bàwk káo wâh cháhn/pŏhm dtâwng yóhk lê(r)k náht บอกเค้าว่าฉัน/ผมต้องยกเลิกนัด

K. Ke(r)-ii bpai Phuket réu yahng káh/kráhp? เคยไปภูเก็ตรึยังคะ/ครับ?

L. Cháhn/pŏhm mâi ke(r)-ii lêhn fóot bawn ฉัน/ผมไม่เคยเล่นฟุตบอล

3) A. Yes : Náht láew kàh/kráhp นัดแล้วค่ะ/ครับ
No : Yahng mâi náht kàh/kráhp ยังไม่นัดค่ะ/ครับ

B. Yes : Mii láew kàh/kráhp มีมาแล้วค่ะ/ครับ
No : Yahng mâi mii kàh/kráhp ยังไม่มีค่ะ/ครับ

C. Yes : Nahn láew kàh/kráhp นานแล้วค่ะ/ครับ
No : Yahng mâi nahn kàh/kráhp ยังไม่นานค่ะ/ครับ

D. Yes : Bàwk láew kàh/kráhp บอกแล้วค่ะ/ครับ
   No : Yahng mâi bàwk kàh/kráhp ยังไม่บอกค่ะ/ครับ
E. Yes : Bpai láew kàh/kráhp ไปแล้วค่ะ/ครับ
   No : Yahng mâi bpai kàh/kráhp ยังไม่ไปค่ะ/ครับ
F. Yes : Dtèun láew kàh/kráhp ตื่นแล้วคะ/ครับ
   No : Yahng mâi dtèun kàh/kráhp ยังไม่ตื่นค่ะ/ครับ
G. Yes : Ngûang láew kàh/kráhp ง่วงแล้วค่ะ/ครับ
   No : Yahng mâi ngûang kàh/kráhp ยังไม่ง่วงค่ะ/ครับ
H. Yes : Gin láew kàh/kráhp กินแล้วค่ะ/ครับ
   No : Yahng mâi gin kàh/kráhp ยังไม่กินค่ะ/ครับ
I: Yes : Hĩw láew kàh/kráhp หิวแล้วค่ะ/ครับ
   No : Yahng mâi hĩw kàh/kráhp ยังไม่หิวค่ะ/ครับ
J: Yes : Ke(r)-ii kàh/kráhp เคยค่ะ/ครับ
   No : Yahng mâi ke(r)-ii kàh/kráhp. ยังไม่เคยค่ะ/ครับ
K: Yes : Ke(r)-ii kàh/kráhp เคยค่ะ/ครับ
   No : Yahng mâi ke(r)-ii kàh/kráhp.ยังไม่เคยค่ะ/ครับ

11. INVITATION

1) A. Rao jàh bpai tîi năi dii? เราจะไปที่ไหนดี?
   B. Rao jàh tahm arai dii? เราจะทำอะไรดี?
   C. Rao jàh je(r) gahn mêua rai dii? เราจะเจอกันเมื่อไรดี?
   D. Rao jàh ráwng plehng tîi năi dii? เราจะร้องเพลงที่ไหนดี?
   E. Rao jàh tahn/gin tîi năi dii? เราจะกิน/ทานที่ไหนดี?
   F. Rao jàh doo năhng (rêuang) arai dii? เราจะดูหนัง(เรื่อง)อะไรดี?
   G. Rao jàh che(r)n krai dii? เราจะเชิญใครดี?

2) A. Bpai tahn/gin ah hăhn glahng wahn dûay gahn mái káh/kráhp? ไปทาน/กินอาหารกลางวันด้วยกันมั้ยคะ/ครับ?
   B. Kàwp koon kàh/kráhp, dtàe bpai mâi dâi, yôong mâhk ขอบคุณค่ะ/ครับแต่ไปไม่ได้ ยุ่งมาก

C. Wahn ah tít wâhng mái káh/kráhp? วันอาทิตย์ว่างมั้ยคะ/ครับ?

D. Di cháhn/pŏhm kăw che(r)n koon bpai ngahn dtàeng ngahn di cháhn/pŏhm nàw-ii kàh/kráhp ดิฉัน/ผมขอเชิญคุณไปงานแต่งงานดิฉัน/ผมหน่อยค่ะ/ครับ

E. Che(r)n nâhng kàh/kráhp เชิญนั่งค่ะ/ครับ

F. Prôong nii bpai lêhn gáwp dûay gahn mái káh/kráhp? พรุ่งนี้ไปเล่นกอล์ฟด้วยกันมั้ยคะ/ครับ?

G. Che(r)n kàh/kráhp เชิญค่ะ/ครับ

12. TELEPHONE CONVERSATION

1) A. Raw sáhk krôo kàh/kráhp รอสักครู่ค่ะ/ครับ

B. Kăw pôot gàhp jim nàw-ii kàh/kráhp ขอพูดกับจิมหน่อยค่ะ/ครับ

C. Chûay bàwk soo sahn hâi toh hăh di cháhn/pŏhm nàw-ii kàh/kráhp ช่วยบอกซูซานให้โทรหาดิฉัน/ผมหน่อยค่ะ/ครับ

D. Meu tĕu koon, be(r) arai káh/kráhp? มือถือคุณเบอร์อะไรคะ/ครับ?

E. Koon toh pìt kàh/kráhp คุณโทรผิดค่ะ/ครับ

F. Chûay toh glàhp (mah) ìik săwng chûa mohng dâi mái káh/kráhp? ช่วยโทรกลับ(มา)อีกสองชั่วโมงได้มั้ยคะ/ครับ?

G. Chûay toh glàhp (mah) dtawn săwng mohng dâi mái káh/kráhp? ช่วยโทรกลับ(มา)ตอนสองโมงได้มั้ยคะ/ครับ?

H. Chûay toh glàhp (mah) dtawn bàh-ii dâi mái káh/kráhp? ช่วยโทรกลับ(มา)ตอนบ่ายได้มั้ยคะ/ครับ?

2) A. Kăw pôot gàhp pôo jàht gahn nàw-ii kàh/kráhp ขอพูดกับผู้จัดการหน่อยค่ะ/ครับ

B. Chûay bàwk káo hâi toh hăh di cháhn/pŏhm tîi be(r) Sŏon săwng săwng săhm sìi hâh hòhk jèht bpàet. ช่วยบอกเค้าให้โทรหาดิฉัน/ผมที่เบอร์ศูนย์ สอง สอง สาม สี่ ห้า หก เจ็ด แปด

C. Káo jàh glàhp (mah) mêua rai káh/kráhp?
เค้าจะกลับ(มา) เมื่อไรคะ/ครับ?
Meu tĕu pôo jàht gahn, be(r) arai káh/kráhp?
มือถือผู้จัดการเบอร์อะไรคะ/ครับ?
D. Di cháhn/pŏhm jàh toh glàhp (bpai) dtawn bàh-ii náh káh/náh kráhp
ดิฉันจะโทรกลับ(ไป)ตอนบ่ายนะคะ/นะครับ

13. HOUSEKEEPING

1) A. Ah hăhn nîi pèht ge(r)n bpai อาหารนี่เผ็ดเกินไป
   B. Ah gàht tîi nîi ráwn mâhk อากาศที่นี่ร้อนมาก
   C. Mii kohn mâhk ge(r)n bpai มีคนมากเกินไป
   D. Jing jing lĕ(r)? จริงๆเหรอ?
   E. Glai jing jing ไกลจริงๆ
   F. Kăwng tîi nîi paeng mâhk ของที่นี่แพงมาก
   G. Kít wâh dĭaw fŏhn jàh dtòhk คิดว่าเดี๋ยวฝนจะตก
   H. Di cháhn/Pŏhm róo wâh prôong níi wahn yòot
      ดิฉัน/ผมรู้ว่า พรุ่งนี้วันหยุด

2) A. Did you hear what he said?
   B. I can't find my wallet.
   C. Did you see him yesterday?
   D. I couldn't sleep last night.
   E. Didn't you meet him just now?
   F. I am really bored.
   G. Could you turn the airconditioner off please?
   H. I know that you want to go out.

14. GROOMING

1) A. Di cháhn/Pŏhm mâi hĭw le(r)-ii ดิฉัน/ผมไม่หิวเลย
   B. Káo mâi nèua-ii le(r)-ii เค้าไม่เหนื่อยเลย
   C. Ao bpàhk gah àwk mah jàhk glàwng
      เอาปากกาออกมาจากกล่อง
   D. Ao wái kráhng nâh, di cháhn/pŏhm jàh àhn เอาไว้ครั้งหน้า ดิฉัน/ผมจะอ่าน
   E. Káo mii pêuan mài เค้ามีเพื่อนใหม่
   F. Pôot mài พูดใหม่
   G. Sêua dtua níi sài (to wear) paw dii เสื้อตัวนี้ใส่พอดี
   H. Di cháhn/pŏhm châwp wâh-ii náhm tîi sòot ดิฉัน/ผมชอบว่าน้ำที่สุด
   I. Koon châwp dtóh dtua năi mâhk gwàh? คุณชอบโต๊ะตัวไหนมากกว่า?

2) A. Kăw bpai dûay dâi mâi káh/kráhp? ขอไปด้วยได้มั้ยคะ/ครับ?
   B. Di cháhn/Pŏhm sŏong gwàh náwng chah-ii, dtàe pîi săh-oo sŏong tîi sòot ดิฉัน/ผมสูงกว่าน้องชาย แต่พี่สาวสูงที่สุด
   C. Kăw kùat mài kàh/kráhp ขอขวดใหม่ค่ะ/ครับ
   D. Kăw doo krêuang tîi dii tîi sòot nàw-ii kàh/kráhp ขอดูเครื่องที่ดีที่สุดหน่อยค่ะ/ครับ
   E. Tahm sĭi pŏhm nàw-ii kàh/kráhp ทำสีผมหน่อยค่ะ/ครับ
   F. Bpai dûay gahn mái káh/kráhp? ไปด้วยกันมั้ยคะ/ครับ?
   G. Che(r)n kàh/kráhp เชิญค่ะ/ครับ
   H. Ao wái kráhng nâh, náh káh/náh kráhp
      เอาไว้ครั้งหน้านะคะ/นะครับ

15. MEDICINE

1) A. Káo năh-oo gâw le(r)-ii bpìt ae เค้าหนาวก็เลยปิดแอร์

B. Káo ráwn gâw le(r)-ii bpè(r)t ae เค้าร้อนก็เลยเปิดแอร์
C. Rao nèua-ii gâw le(r)-ii yòot nèung wahn
   เราเหนื่อยก็เลยหยุดหนึ่งวัน
D. Hâwng mêut di cháhn/pŏhm gâw le(r)-ii bpè(r)t fai
   ห้องมืด ดิฉัน/ผมก็เลยเปิดไฟ
E. Di cháhn/pŏhm mii bpràh choom gâw le(r)-ii dtâwng dtèun cháh-oo ดิฉัน/ผมมีประชุมก็เลยต้องตื่นเช้า
F. Wìt tah yóo sĭa gâw le(r)-ii mâi dâi fahng kàh-oo วิทยุเสียก็เลยไม่ได้ฟังข่าว
G. Gràh bpăo (bai) níi mâi paeng, di cháhn/pŏhm gâw le(r)-ii yàhk séu กระเป๋า(ใบ)นี้ไม่แพงผมก็เลยอยากซื้อ
H. Róht dtìt mâhk, di cháhn/pŏhm gâw le(r)-ii pìt náht
   รถติดมากดิฉัน/ผมก็เลยผิดนัด
I. Di cháhn/pŏhm mâi dâi yin sĭang toh rah sàhp gâw le(r)-ii mâi dâi ráhp toh rah sàhp
   ดิฉัน/ผมไม่ได้ยินเสียงโทรศัพท์ก็เลยไม่ได้รับโทรศัพท์

2) A. Nîi gi loh láh tâo rai káh/kráhp? นี่กิโลละเท่าไรคะ/ครับ?
   B. Di cháhn/pŏhm bpai tîi nâhn ah tít láh săhm kráhng
      ดิฉัน/ผมไปที่นั่นอาทิตย์ละสามครั้ง
   C. Di cháhn/pŏhm àwk gahm lahng gah-ii kráhng láh sìi sìp hâh nah tii ดิฉัน/ผมออกกำลังกายครั้งละสี่สิบห้านาที
   D. Káo hâi di cháhn/pŏhm glàhp bâhn เค้าให้ดิฉัน/ผมกลับบ้าน
   E. Krai hâi koon nâhng? ใครให้คุณนั่ง?
   F. Káo mâi dâi hâi koon toh hăh di cháhn/pŏhm เค้าไม่ได้ให้คุณโทรหาดิฉัน/ผม
   G. Mâi mii krai yòo ไม่มีใครอยู่
   H. Mâi mii tîi năi tòok ไม่มีที่ไหนถูก
   I. Mâi mii arai (yòo) bohn dtóh ไม่มี(อยู่)อะไรบนโต๊ะ

3) A. Dii kêun kàh/kráhp ดีขึ้นค่ะ/ครับ
   B. Bpehn arai káh/kráhp? เป็นอะไรคะ/ครับ?
   C. Mâi dâi bpehn arai kàh/kráhp ไม่ได้เป็นอะไรค่ะ/ครับ
   D. Mah groong têhp bpii láh gìi kráhng káh/kráhp? มากรุงเทพปีละกี่ครั้งคะ/ครับ?
   E. Koon jim hâi/sòhng koon mah lĕ(r) káh/kráhp? คุณจิมให้/ส่งคุณมาเหรอคะ/ครับ?
   F. Kăw/ao yah gâe ai nàw-ii kàh/kráhp ขอ/เอายาแก้ไอหน่อยค่ะ/ครับ

4) A. You look better (more beautiful).
   B. Take medicine four times a day.
   C. My mother asked me to come and pick-up a book.
   D. When I am very hungry, I like to come and eat here.
   E. He was not there, therefore I couldn't come.
   F. Nothing in the bag.
   G. Nobody answers the phone today.

16. PETTY-CRIME

1) A. Káo lâo hâi di cháhn/pŏhm fahng wâh káo hĕhn koon mêua wahn níi เค้าเล่าให้ดิฉัน/ผมฟังว่าเค้าเห็นคุณเมื่อวานนี้
   B. Mii kùat èun mái káh/kráhp? มีขวดอื่นมั้ยคะ/ครับ?
   C. Gèhp gràh dàht wái bohn dtóh เก็บกระดาษไว้บนโต๊ะ
   D. Koon róo mái wâh káo gèhp goon jae wái tîi năi? คุณรู้มั้ยว่า เค้าเก็บกุญแจไว้ที่ไหน?
   E. Rao lŏhng tahng เราหลงทาง
   F. Koon tahm toh rah sàhp sĭa คุณทำโทรศัพท์เสีย
   G. Káo tòok bplôhn เค้าถูกปล้น
   H. Jahn dtàek จานแตก

2) A. He/She is very tall.
   B. He/she is short and chubby.
   C. Long hair, wearing a red shirt.
   D. A thin woman wearing black shoes.
   E. A short man, not fat, not thin.
   F. A person in her/his forties.
   G. Not short, not very tall.
   H. Not very old.

About the Author

Khun Rungrat Luanwarawat has been working in the language field for more than a decade. Prior to becoming a Thai language instructor she worked as a translator, writer, journalist and English teacher. Her most recent project involved the development of an award-winning Thai language textbook for a major diplomatic mission in Bangkok; this accomplishment represents a prime example of her innovative approach to linguistics training.

Apart from teaching, she also coordinates language and cultural field trips for embassy officials. She is a co-founder of Thai Country Trails (*www.thaicountrytrails.com*), a pioneering business that merges the fields of language and cultural training, and travel.